jQuery
Pocket Reference

jQuery
Pocket Reference

David Flanagan

O'REILLY®

Beijing · Cambridge · Farnham · Köln · Sebastopol · Tokyo

jQuery Pocket Reference
by David Flanagan

Published by O'Reilly Media, Inc., 1005 Gravenstein Highway North, Sebastopol, CA 95472.

O'Reilly books may be purchased for educational, business, or sales promotional use. Online editions are also available for most titles (*http://my.safari booksonline.com*). For more information, contact our corporate/institutional sales department: (800) 998-9938 or *corporate@oreilly.com*.

Editors: Mike Loukides and Simon St. Laurent
Production Editor: Teresa Elsey
Proofreader: Marlowe Shaeffer
Indexer: Ellen Troutman Zaig
Cover Designer: Karen Montgomery
Interior Designer: David Futato

Printing History:
　　December 2010:　　　First Edition.

ISBN: 978-1-449-39722-7

[TG]

1291651155

Contents

Preface

This book covers version 1.4 of the jQuery library for client-side JavaScript programming. It is one chapter from my much longer book *JavaScript: The Definitive Guide*. jQuery is such a powerful library and so well suited to pocket reference format that it seemed worth publishing this material on its own.

This book assumes that you already know how to program with JavaScript, and that you are familiar with the basics of client-side JavaScript programming without jQuery. For example, you should know about DOM methods like `getElement ById()`, `getElementsByTagName()`, and `addEventListener()`.

Thanks to Raffaele Cecco for a timely and thorough review of the book and of the code it contains. Thanks also to John Resig and the entire jQuery team for creating such a useful library, to my editor Mike Loukides for his enthusiasm for this project, and to the O'Reilly production department for getting this book out so quickly.

The examples in this book can be downloaded from the book's web page, which will also include errata if any errors are discovered after publication:

http://oreilly.com/catalog/0636920016182/

In general, you may use the examples in this book in your programs and documentation. You do not need to contact us for permission unless you're reproducing a significant portion of the code. We appreciate, but do not require, an attribution like this: "From *jQuery Pocket Reference* by David Flanagan (O'Reilly). Copyright 2011 David Flanagan, 978-1-449-39722-7." If you feel your use of code examples falls outside fair use or the permission given here, feel free to contact us at *permissions@oreilly.com*.

To comment or ask technical questions about this book, send email to:

    bookquestions@oreilly.com

This book is also available from the Safari Books Online service. For full digital access to this book and others on similar topics from O'Reilly and other publishers, sign up at *http://my.safaribooksonline.com*.

CHAPTER 1

Introduction to jQuery

JavaScript has an intentionally simple core API and an overly complicated client-side API that is marred by major incompatibilities between browsers. The arrival of IE9 eliminates the worst of those incompatibilities, but many programmers find it easier to write web applications using a JavaScript framework or utility library to simplify common tasks and hide the differences between browsers. At the time of this writing, jQuery is one of the most popular and widely used of these libraries.

Because it has become so widely used, web developers should be familiar with the jQuery library: even if you don't use it in your own code, you are likely to encounter it in code written by others. Fortunately, jQuery is stable and small enough to document in pocket reference form.

jQuery makes it easy to find the elements of a document, and then manipulate those elements by adding content, editing HTML attributes and CSS properties, defining event handlers, and performing animations. It also has Ajax utilities for dynamically making HTTP requests, and general-purpose utility functions for working with objects and arrays.

As its name implies, the jQuery library is focused on *queries*. A typical query uses a CSS selector to identify a set of document elements and then returns an object that represents those elements. This returned object provides many useful methods for operating on the matching elements as a group. Whenever possible, these methods return the object on which they are invoked, allowing a succinct method-chaining idiom to be used. These features are at the heart of jQuery's power and utility:

- An expressive syntax (CSS selectors) for referring to elements in the document
- An efficient query method for finding the set of document elements that match a CSS selector
- A useful set of methods for manipulating selected elements
- Powerful functional programming techniques for operating on sets of elements as a group, rather than one at a time
- A succinct idiom (method chaining) for expressing sequences of operations

This book begins with an introduction to jQuery that shows how to make simple queries and work with the results. The chapters that follow explain:

- How to set HTML attributes; CSS styles and classes; HTML form values; and element content, geometry, and data
- How to alter the structure of a document by inserting, replacing, wrapping, and deleting elements
- How to use jQuery's cross-browser event model
- How to produce animated visual effects with jQuery
- jQuery's Ajax utilities for making scripted HTTP requests
- jQuery's utility functions
- The full syntax of jQuery's selectors, and how to use jQuery's advanced selection methods
- How to extend jQuery by using and writing plugins
- The jQuery UI library

The end of this book is a quick reference to all of jQuery's methods and functions.

jQuery Basics

The jQuery library defines a single global function named jQuery(). This function is so frequently used that the library also defines the global symbol $ as a shortcut for it. These are the only two symbols jQuery defines in the global namespace.*

This single global function with two names is the central query function for jQuery. Here, for example, is how we ask for the set of all <div> tags in a document:

```
var divs = $("div");
```

The value returned by this function represents a set of zero or more DOM elements and is known as a jQuery object. Note that jQuery() is a factory function rather than a constructor: it returns a newly created object, but it is not used with the new keyword. jQuery objects define many methods for operating on the sets of elements they represent, and most of this book is devoted to explaining those methods. Below, for example, is code that finds, highlights, and quickly displays all hidden <p> tags that have a class of "more":

```
$("p.more").css("background-color", "gray").show("fast");
```

The css() method operates on the jQuery object returned by $(), and returns that same object so that the show() method can be invoked next in a compact "method chain". This method-chaining idiom is common in jQuery programming. As another example, the code below finds all elements in the document that have the CSS class "hide", and registers an event handler on each one. That event handler is invoked when the user clicks on the element, making it slowly "slide up" and disappear:

```
$(".hide").click(function() { $(this).slideUp("slow"); });
```

---

* If you use $ in your own code, or are using another library—such as Prototype—that uses $, you can call jQuery.noConflict() to restore $ to its original value.

Obtaining jQuery

The jQuery library is free software you can download from *http://jquery.com*. Once you have the code, you can include it in your web pages with a `<script>` tag:

```
<script src="jquery-1.4.4.min.js"></script>
```

At the time of this writing, the current version of jQuery is 1.4.4. The "min" in the filename above indicates that this is the minimized version of the library, with unnecessary comments and whitespace removed, and internal identifiers replaced with shorter ones.

Another way to use jQuery in your web applications is to allow a content distribution network to serve it using a URL like one of these:

http://code.jquery.com/jquery-1.4.4.min.js

http://ajax.microsoft.com/ajax/jquery/jquery-1.4.4.min.js

http://ajax.googleapis.com/ajax/libs/jquery/1.4.4/jquery.min.js

Replace the "1.4.4" version number in the URLs above as necessary. If you use the Google CDN, you can use "1.4" to get the latest release in the 1.4.x series, or just "1" to get the most current release less than 2.0. The major advantage of loading jQuery from well-known URLs like these is that because of jQuery's popularity, visitors to your website will likely already have a copy of the library in their browser's cache and no download will be necessary.

The jQuery() Function

The `jQuery()` function (a.k.a. `$()`) is the most important one in the jQuery library. It is heavily overloaded, however, and there are four different ways you can invoke it.

The first and most common way to invoke `$()` is to pass a CSS selector (a string) to it. When called this way, it returns the set of elements from the current document that match the selector.

jQuery supports most of the CSS3 selector syntax, plus some extensions of its own. Complete details of the jQuery selector syntax are in "jQuery Selectors" on page 89. If you pass an element or a jQuery object as the second argument to $(), it returns only matching descendants of the specified element (or elements). This optional second argument value defines the starting point (or points) for the query and is often called the *context*.

The second way to invoke $() is to pass it an Element, Document, or Window object. Called like this, it simply wraps the element, document, or window in a jQuery object and returns that object, allowing you to use jQuery methods to manipulate the element rather than using raw DOM methods. It is common to see jQuery programs call $(document) or $(this), for example. jQuery objects can represent more than one element in a document, and you can also pass an array of elements to $(). In this case, the returned jQuery object represents the set of elements in your array.

The third way to invoke $() is to pass it a string of HTML text. When you do this, jQuery creates the HTML element (or elements) described by that text and then returns a jQuery object representing those elements. jQuery does not automatically insert the newly created elements into the document, but the jQuery methods described in Chapter 3 allow you to easily insert them where you want them. Note that you cannot pass plain text when you invoke $() in this way, or jQuery will think you are passing a CSS selector. For this style of invocation, the string you pass to $() must include at least one HTML tag with angle brackets.

When invoked in this third way, $() accepts an optional second argument. You can pass a Document object to specify the document with which the elements are to be associated. (If you are creating elements to be inserted into an <iframe>, for example, you'll need to explicitly specify the Document object of that frame.) Or, you can pass a second argument that specifies the names and values of attributes to set on the newly created elements as an object:

```
var img = $("<img/>",      // Create a new <img> tag
            { src:url,      // With this src attribute
              alt:desc });  // And this alt attribute
```

Finally, the fourth way to invoke $() is to pass a function to it. If you do this, the function you pass will be invoked when the document has been loaded and the DOM is ready to be manipulated. It is very common to see jQuery programs written as anonymous functions defined within a call to jQuery():

```
jQuery(function() { // Invoked when document has loaded
    // All jQuery code goes here
});
```

You'll sometimes see $(f) written using the older and more verbose form: $(document).ready(f).

The function you pass to jQuery() will be invoked with the document object as its **this** value and with the jQuery function as its single argument. This means that you can undefine the global $ function and still use that convenient alias locally with this idiom:

```
jQuery.noConflict();  // Restore $ to its original state
jQuery(function($) {
    // Use $ as a local alias for the jQuery object
    // Put all your jQuery code here
});
```

jQuery triggers functions registered through $() when the "DOMContentLoaded" event is fired, or, in browsers that don't support that event, when the "load" event is fired. This means that the document will be completely parsed, but that external resources such as images may not be loaded yet. If you pass a function to $() after the DOM is ready, that function will be invoked immediately—before $() returns.

The jQuery library also uses the jQuery() function as its namespace, and defines a number of utility functions and properties under it. The jQuery.noConflict() function mentioned above is one such utility function. Others include jQuery.each() for general-purpose iteration and jQuery.parseJSON() for parsing JSON text. Chapter 7 lists general-purpose utility

---

functions, and other jQuery functions are described throughout this book.

jQuery Terminology

Let's pause here to define some important terms and phrases that you'll see throughout this book:

"the jQuery function"
> The jQuery function is the value of `jQuery` or of `$`. This is the function that creates jQuery objects and registers handlers to be invoked when the DOM is ready; it also serves as the jQuery namespace. I usually refer to it as `$()`. Because it serves as a namespace, the jQuery function might also be called "the global jQuery object", but it is very important not to confuse it with "a jQuery object".

"a jQuery object"
> A jQuery object is an object returned by the jQuery function. A jQuery object represents a set of document elements and can also be called a "jQuery result", a "jQuery set", or a "wrapped set".

"the selected elements"
> When you pass a CSS selector to the jQuery function, it returns a jQuery object that represents the set of document elements matching that selector. When describing the methods of the jQuery object, I'll often use the phrase "the selected elements" to refer to those matching elements. For example, to explain the `attr()` method, I might write, "the `attr()` method sets HTML attributes on the selected elements", rather than a more precise but awkward description like, "the `attr()` method sets HTML attributes on the elements of the jQuery object on which it was invoked". Note that the word "selected" refers to the CSS selector and has nothing to do with any selection performed by the user.

"a jQuery function"
> This is a function like `jQuery.noConflict()` that is defined in the namespace of *the* jQuery function. jQuery functions might also be described as "static methods".

"a jQuery method"

> A jQuery method is a method of a jQuery object returned by the jQuery function. The most important part of the jQuery library is the powerful methods it defines.

The distinction between jQuery functions and methods is sometimes tricky because a number of functions and methods have the same name. Note the differences between these two lines of code:

```
// Call the jQuery function each() to invoke the
// function f once for each element of the array a
$.each(a,f);

// Call the jQuery() function to obtain a jQuery
// object that represents all <a> elements in the
// document. Then call the each() method of that
// jQuery object to invoke the function f once for
// each selected element.
$("a").each(f);
```

The official jQuery documentation at *http://jquery.com* uses names like $.each to refer to jQuery functions, and names like .each (with a period but without a dollar sign) to refer to jQuery methods. In this book, I'll use the term "function" and "method" instead. Usually it will be clear from the context that is being discussed.

Queries and Query Results

When you pass a jQuery selector string to $(), it returns a jQuery object that represents the set of matched (or "selected") elements. jQuery selectors are very much like the CSS selectors you use in stylesheets. For example:

```
div          // all <div> elements
#surname     // the element with id="surname"
.warning     // all elements with class="warning"
```

$() vs. querySelectorAll()

The $() function is similar to the Document method
querySelectorAll(): both take a CSS selector as their argument
and return an array-like object that holds the elements that
match the selector. The jQuery implementation uses
querySelectorAll() in browsers that support it, but there are
good reasons to use $() instead of querySelectorAll() in your
own code:

- querySelectorAll() has only recently been implemented
  by browser vendors, whereas $() works in older browsers
  as well as new ones.

- Because jQuery can perform selections "by hand", the
  CSS3 selectors supported by $() work in all browsers, not
  just those browsers that support CSS3.

- The array-like object returned by $() (a jQuery object) is
  much more useful than the array-like object (a NodeList)
  returned by querySelectorAll().

The specific selector syntax supported by jQuery is detailed in
"jQuery Selectors" on page 89. Rather than focus on those
advanced selector details now, we're going to first explore what
you can do with the results of a query.

The value returned by $() is a jQuery object. jQuery objects
are array-like: they have a length property and numeric properties from 0 to length-1. This means that you can access the
contents of the jQuery object using standard square-bracket
array notation:

```
$("body").length  // => 1: documents have only one body
$("body")[0]      // This the same as document.body
```

If you prefer not to use array notation with jQuery objects, you
can use the size() method instead of the length property, and
the get() method instead of indexing with square brackets. If
you need to convert a jQuery object to a true array, call the
toArray() method.

In addition to the `length` property, jQuery objects have three other properties that are sometimes of interest. The `selector` property is the selector string (if any) that was used when the jQuery object was created. The `context` property is the context object that was passed as the second argument to `$()`, or the Document object otherwise. Finally, all jQuery objects have a property named `jquery`, and testing for the existence of this property is a simple way to distinguish jQuery objects from other array-like objects. The value of the `jquery` property is the jQuery version number as a string:

```
// Find all <script> elements in the document body
var bodyscripts = $("script", document.body);
bodyscripts.selector   // => "script"
bodyscripts.context    // => document.body
bodyscripts.jquery     // => "1.4.2"
```

If you want to loop over all elements in a jQuery object, call the `each()` method instead of writing a `for` loop. The `each()` method is something like the ECMAScript 5 (ES5) `forEach()` array method. It expects a callback function as its sole argument, and invokes that callback function once for each element in the jQuery object (in document order). The callback is invoked as a method of the matched element, so within the callback the `this` keyword refers to an Element object. `each()` also passes the index and the element as the first and second arguments to the callback. Note that `this` and the second argument are raw document elements, not jQuery objects; if you want to use a jQuery method to manipulate the element, you'll need to pass it to `$()` first.

jQuery's `each()` method has one feature that is quite different than `forEach()`: if your callback returns `false` for any element, iteration is terminated after that element (this is like using the `break` keyword in a normal loop). `each()` returns the jQuery object on which it is called so that it can be used in method chains. Here is an example (it uses the `prepend()` method that will be explained in Chapter 3):

```
// Number the divs of the document, up to div#last
$("div").each(function(idx) { // Invoke for each <div>
    // Create a jQuery object from the element
```

```
        // And insert the index at start of it.
        $(this).prepend(idx + ": ");
        // Stop iterating when we reach #last
        if (this.id === "last")
            return false;
});
```

Despite the power of the each() method, it is not very commonly used since jQuery methods usually iterate implicitly over the set of matched elements and operate on them all. You typically only need to use each() if you need to manipulate the matched elements in different ways. Even then, you may not need to call each() since a number of jQuery methods allow you to pass a callback function.

The jQuery library predates the ES5 array methods and defines a couple of other methods that provide similar functionality. The jQuery method map() works much like the Array.map() method. It accepts a callback function as its argument and invokes that function once for each element of the jQuery object, collecting the return values of those invocations, and returning a new jQuery object holding those return values. map() invokes the callback in the same way as the each() method: the element is passed as the this value and as the second argument, and the index of the element is passed as the first argument. If the callback returns null or undefined, that value is ignored and nothing is added to the new jQuery object for that invocation. If the callback returns an array or an array-like object (such as a jQuery object), it is "flattened" and its elements are added individually to the new jQuery object. Note that the jQuery object returned by map() may not hold document elements, but it still works as an array-like object. Here is an example:

```
$(":header")                    // Find all headings.
    .map(function() {           // Map them to
        return this.id; // their ids.
    })
    .toArray()                  // Convert to a true array
    .sort();                    // And sort that array
```

Along with each() and map(), another fundamental jQuery method is index(). This method expects an element as its argument, and it returns the index of that element in the jQuery object, or -1 if it is not found. In typical jQuery fashion, however, this index() method is overloaded. If you pass a jQuery object as the argument, index() searches for the first element of that object. If you pass a string, index() uses it as a CSS selector and returns the index of the first element of this jQuery object in the set of elements matching that selector. And if you pass no argument, index() returns the index of the first element within its sibling elements.

The final general-purpose jQuery method we'll discuss here is is(). It takes a selector as its argument and returns true if at least one of the selected elements also matches the specified selector. You might use it in an each() callback function, for example:

```
$("div").each(function() {      // For each <div> element
    if ($(this).is(":hidden")) // Skip hidden elements
        return;
    // Do something with the visible ones here
});
```

CHAPTER 2

Element Getters and Setters

Some of the simplest and most common operations on jQuery objects are those that get or set the value of HTML attributes, CSS styles, element content, or element geometry. This chapter describes those methods. First, however, it is worth making some generalizations about getter and setter methods in jQuery:

- Rather than defining a pair of methods, jQuery uses a single method as both getter and setter. If you pass a new value to the method, it sets that value; if you don't specify a value, it returns the current value.

- When used as setters, these methods set values on every element in the jQuery object and then return the jQuery object to allow method chaining.

- When used as a getter, these methods query only the first element of the set of elements and return a single value. (Use `map()` if you want to query all elements.) Since getters do not return the jQuery object they are invoked on, they can only appear at the end of a method chain.

- When used as setters, these methods often accept object arguments. In this case, each property of the object specifies a name and a value to be set.

- When used as setters, these methods often accept functions as values. In this case, the function is invoked to compute the value to be set. The element that the value is being computed for is the `this` value: the element index is passed as the first argument to the function, and the current value is passed as the second argument.

Keep these generalizations about getters and setters in mind as you read the rest of this chapter. Each section below explains an important category of jQuery getter/setter methods.

Getting and Setting HTML Attributes

The `attr()` method is the jQuery getter/setter for HTML attributes, and it adheres to each of the generalizations described above. `attr()` handles browser incompatibilities and special cases, and allows you to use either HTML attribute names or their JavaScript property equivalents (where they differ). For example, you can use either "for" or "htmlFor", and either "class" or "className". `removeAttr()` is a related function that completely removes an attribute from all selected elements. Here are some examples:

```
// Query the action attr of 1st form
$("form").attr("action");
// Set the src attribute of element with id icon
$("#icon").attr("src", "icon.gif");
// Set 4 attributes at once
$("#banner").attr({src:"banner.gif",
                   alt:"Advertisement",
                   width:720, height:64});
// Make all links load in new windows
$("a").attr("target", "_blank");
// Compute the target attribute to load local links
// locally and load off-site links in a new window
$("a").attr("target", function() {
    if (this.host == location.host) return "_self"
    else return "_blank";
});
// We can also pass functions like this
$("a").attr({target: function() {...}});
// Make all links load in this window
$("a").removeAttr("target");
```

`attr()` is jQuery's master attribute-setting function, and you can use it to set things other than normal HTML attributes. If you use the `attr()` method to set an attribute named "css", "val", "html", "text", "data", "width", "height", or "offset", jQuery invokes the method that has the same name as that attribute and passes whatever value you specified as the argument. For example, calling `attr("css", {background Color:"gray"})` is the same as calling `css({background Color:"gray"})`. We'll learn about `css()`, `val()`, `html()`, and other methods in the sections that follow. Note that `attr()` has this behavior when you pass one of these special attribute names as the first argument, and also when these attribute names are used as property names in an object.

Getting and Setting CSS Attributes

The `css()` method is very much like the `attr()` method, but it works with the CSS styles of an element rather than the HTML attributes of the element. When querying style values, `css()` returns the current style (or "computed style") of the element: the returned value may come from the **style** attribute or from a stylesheet. Note that it is not possible to query compound styles such as "font" or "margin". You must instead query individual styles such as "font-weight", "font-family", "margin-top", and "margin-left". When setting styles, the `css()` method simply adds the style to the element's **style** attribute. `css()` allows you to use hyphenated CSS style names ("background-color") or camel-case JavaScript style names ("background-Color"). When querying style values, `css()` returns numeric values as strings, with the units suffix included. When setting, however, it converts numbers to strings and adds a "px" (pixels) suffix to them when necessary:

```
$("h1").css("font-weight"); // Get font weight of 1st <h1>
$("h1").css("fontWeight");  // Camel case works, too
$("h1").css("font"); // ERROR: can't query compound style
$("h1").css("font-variant", // Set style on all <h1> tags
            "smallcaps");
$("div.note").css("border", // Okay to set compound styles
```

```
                         "solid black 2px");
// Set multiple styles at once
$("h1").css({ backgroundColor: "black",
              textColor: "white",
              fontVariant: "small-caps",
              padding: "10px 2px 4px 20px",
              border: "dotted black 4px" });
// Increase all <h1> font sizes by 25%
$("h1").css("font-size", function(i,curval) {
            return Math.round(1.25*parseInt(curval));
          });
```

Getting and Setting CSS Classes

Recall that the value of the class attribute (accessed via the
className property in JavaScript) is interpreted as a space-
separated list of CSS class names. Usually, we want to add,
remove, or test for the presence of a single name in the list
rather than replace one list of classes with another. For this
reason, jQuery defines convenience methods for working with
the class attribute. addClass() and removeClass() add and remove classes from the selected elements. toggleClass() adds
classes to elements that don't already have them, and removes
classes from those that do. hasClass() tests for the presence of
a specified class. Here are some examples:

```
// Add a CSS class to all <h1> tags
$("h1").addClass("hilite");
// Add 2 classes to <p> tags after <h1>
$("h1+p").addClass("hilite firstpara");
// Pass a function to add a computed class to each elt.
$("section").addClass(function(n) {
    return "section" + n;
});

// Remove a class from all <p> tags
$("p").removeClass("hilite");
// Multiple classes are allowed
$("p").removeClass("hilite firstpara");
// Remove computed classes from tags
$("section").removeClass(function(n) {
    return "section" + n;
});
```

```
// Remove all classes from all <div>s
$("div").removeClass();

// Toggle a CSS class: add the class if it is not
// there or remove it if it is.
$("tr:odd").toggleClass("oddrow");
// Toggle two classes at once
$("h1").toggleClass("big bold");
// Toggle a computed class or classes
$("h1").toggleClass(function(n) {
    return "big bold h1-" + n;
});
$("h1").toggleClass("hilite", true);  // Like addClass
$("h1").toggleClass("hilite", false); // Like removeClass

// Testing for CSS classes: does any <p> have this class?
$("p").hasClass("firstpara")
// This does the same thing.
$("#lead").is(".firstpara")
// is() is more flexible than hasClass()
$("#lead").is(".firstpara.hilite")
```

Note that the hasClass() method is less flexible than add
Class(), removeClass(), and toggleClass(). hasClass() works
for only a single class name and does not support function arguments. It returns true if any of the selected elements has the
specified CSS class, and it returns false if none of them does.
The is() method (described in "Queries and Query Results" on page 8) is more flexible and can be used for the same
purpose.

These jQuery methods are like the methods of the HTML5
classList property. But the jQuery methods work in all browsers, not just those that support HTML5. Also, of course, the
jQuery methods work for multiple elements and can be
chained.

Getting and Setting HTML Form Values

val() is a method for setting and querying the value attribute
of HTML form elements, and also for querying and setting the

selection state of checkboxes, radio buttons, and <select> elements:

```
// Get value from the surname text field
$("#surname").val()
// Get single value from <select>
$("#usstate").val()
// Get array of values from <select multiple>
$("select#extras").val()
// Get val of checked radio button
$("input:radio[name=ship]:checked").val()
// Set value of a text field
$("#email").val("Invalid email address")
// Check any checkboxes with these names or values
$("input:checkbox").val(["opt1", "opt2"])
// Reset all text fields to their default
$("input:text").val(function() {
    return this.defaultValue;
})
```

Getting and Setting Element Content

The text() and html() methods query and set the plain-text or HTML content of an element. When invoked with no arguments, text() returns the plain-text content of all descendant text nodes of all matched elements. This works even in browsers that do not support the textContent or innerText properties.

If you invoke the html() method with no arguments, it returns the HTML content of just the first matched element. jQuery uses the innerHTML property to do this: x.html() is effectively the same as x[0].innerHTML.

If you pass a string to text() or html(), that string will be used for the plain-text or HTML-formatted text content of the element, and it will replace all existing content. As with the other setter methods we've seen, you can also pass a function, which will be used to compute the new content string:

```
var t = $("head title").text(); // Get document title
var hdr = $("h1").html()        // Get html of first <h1>
// Give each heading a section number
```

```
$("h1").text(function(n, current) {
    return "§" + (n+1) + ": " + current
});
```

Getting and Setting Element Geometry

It can be tricky to correctly determine the size and position of an element, especially in browsers that do not support `getBoundingClientRect()`. jQuery simplifies these computations with methods that work in any browser. Note that all of the methods described here are getters, but only some can also be used as setters.

To query or set the position of an element, use the `offset()` method. This method measures positions relative to the document, and returns them in the form of an object with `left` and `top` properties that hold the X and Y coordinates. If you pass an object with these properties to the method, it sets the position you specify. It sets the CSS `position` attribute as necessary to make elements positionable:

```
var elt = $("#sprite"); // The element we want to move
var pos = elt.offset(); // Get its current position
pos.top += 100;         // change the Y coordinate
elt.offset(pos);        // Set the new position

// Move all <h1> tags to the right by a distance
// that depends on their position in the document.
$("h1").offset(function(index,curpos) {
    return {
        left: curpos.left + 25*index,
        top:curpos.top
    };
});
```

The `position()` method is like `offset()` except that it is a getter only, and it returns element positions relative to their offset parent, rather than to the document as a whole. In the DOM, every element has an `offsetParent` property to which its position is relative. Positioned elements always serve as the offset parents for their descendants, but some browsers also make other elements, such as table cells, into offset parents. jQuery only considers positioned elements to be offset parents, and the `offsetParent()` method of a jQuery object maps each element to the nearest positioned ancestor element or to the `<body>` element. Note the unfortunate naming mismatch for these methods: `offset()` returns the absolute position of an element, in document coordinates; `position()` returns the offset of an element relative to its `offsetParent()`.

There are three getters for querying the width of an element and three for querying the height. The `width()` and `height()` methods return the basic width and height and do not include padding, borders, or margins. `innerWidth()` and `innerHeight()` return the width and height of an element plus the width and height of its padding (the word "inner" refers to the fact that these methods return the dimensions measured to the inside of the border). `outerWidth()` and `outerHeight()` normally return the element's dimensions plus its padding and border. If you pass the value `true` to either of these methods, they also add in the size of the element's margins. The code below shows four different widths that you can compute for an element:

```
var body = $("body");
// Four different widths, depending on what's included
var contentWidth = body.width();
var paddingWidth = body.innerWidth();
var borderWidth = body.outerWidth();
var marginWidth = body.outerWidth(true);
// Sums of the l and r padding, borders, and margins
var padding = paddingWidth-contentWidth;
var borders = borderWidth-paddingWidth;
var margins = marginWidth-borderWidth;
```

The `width()` and `height()` methods have features that the other four methods (inner and outer) do not. One feature is that if the first element of the jQuery object is a Window or Document object, it returns the size of the window's viewport or the full size of the document. The other methods only work for elements, not windows or documents.

The other feature of the `width()` and `height()` methods is that they are setters as well as getters. If you pass a value to these

methods, they set the width or height of every element in the
jQuery object. (Note, however, that they cannot set the width
or height of Window and Document objects.) If you pass a
number, it is taken as a dimension in pixels. If you pass a string
value, it is used as the value of the CSS width or height attribute
and can therefore use any CSS unit. Finally, as with other setters, you can pass a function, which will be called to compute
the width or height.

There is a minor asymmetry between the getter and setter behavior of width() and height(). When used as getters, these
methods return the dimensions of an element's content box,
excluding padding, borders, and margins. When you use them
as setters, however, they simply set the CSS width and height
attributes. By default, those attributes also specify the size of
the content box. But if an element has its CSS box-sizing attribute set to border-box, the width() and height() methods
set dimensions that include the padding and border. For an
element e that uses the content-box model, calling
$(e).width(x).width() returns the value x. For elements that
use the border-box model, however, this is not generally the
case.

The final pair of geometry-related jQuery methods are scroll
Top() and scrollLeft(), which query the scrollbar positions
for an element or set the scrollbar positions for all elements.
These methods work for the Window object as well as for
document elements, and when invoked on a Document, they
query or set the scrollbar positions of the Window that holds
the document. Unlike other setters, you cannot pass a function
to scrollTop() or scrollLeft().

We can use scrollTop() as a getter and a setter, along with the
height() method to define a method that scrolls the window
up or down by the number of pages you specify:

```
// Scroll the window by n pages.
// n may be fractional or negative.
function page(n) {
    // Wrap the window in a jQuery object
    var w = $(window);
```

```
// Get the size of a page
var pagesize = w.height();
// Get the current scrollbar position
var current = w.scrollTop();
// Set new scrollbar position n pages down
w.scrollTop(current + n*pagesize);
}
```

Getting and Setting Element Data

jQuery defines a getter/setter method named `data()` that sets
or queries data associated with any document element or with
the Document or Window object. The ability to associate data
with any element is important and powerful: it is the basis for
jQuery's event handler registration, effecting queuing mecha-
nisms. You may sometimes want to use the `data()` method in
your own code.

To associate data with the elements in a jQuery object, call
`data()` as a setter method, passing a name and a value as the
two arguments. Alternatively, you can pass a single object to
the `data()` setter and each property of that object will be used
as a name/value pair to associate with the element or elements
of the jQuery object. Note, however, that when you pass an
object to `data()`, the properties of that object replace any data
previously associated with the element. Unlike many of the
other setter methods we've seen, `data()` does not invoke functions you pass. If you pass a function as the second argument
to `data()`, that function is stored, just as any other value
would be.

The `data()` method can also serve as a getter, of course. When
invoked with no arguments, it returns an object containing all
name/value pairs associated with the first element in the
jQuery object. When you invoke `data()` with a single string
argument, it returns the value associated with that string for
the first element.

Use the `removeData()` method to remove data from an element.
(Using `data()` to set a named value to `null` or `undefined` is not

the same thing as actually deleting the named value.) If you pass a string to removeData(), the method deletes any value associated with that string for the element. If you call remove Data() with no arguments, it removes all data associated with the element.

```
$("div").data("x", 1);            // Set some data
$("div.nodata").removeData("x");  // Remove some data
var x = $('#mydiv').data("x");    // Query some data
```

jQuery also defines utility function forms of the data() and removeData() methods. You can associate data with an individual element e using either the method or function form of data():

```
$(e).data(...)   // The method form
$.data(e, ...)   // The function form
```

jQuery's data framework does not store element data as properties of the elements themselves, but it does need to add one special property to any element that has data associated with it. Some browsers do not allow properties to be added to <applet>, <object>, and <embed> elements, so jQuery simply does not allow data to be associated with these elements.

CHAPTER 3

Altering Document Structure

In "Getting and Setting Element Content" on page 18 we saw the `html()` and `text()` methods for setting element content. HTML documents are represented as a tree of nodes rather than a linear sequence of characters, so insertions, deletions, and replacements are not as simple as they are for strings and arrays. The sections that follow explain the various jQuery methods for more complex document modification.

Inserting and Replacing Elements

Let's begin with basic methods for insertions and replacements. Each of the methods demonstrated below takes an argument that specifies the content that is to be inserted into the document. This can be a string of plain text or of HTML, or it can be a jQuery object, Element, or text node. The insertion is made into, before, after, or in place of (depending on the method) each of the selected elements. If the content to be inserted is an element that already exists in the document, it is moved from its current location. If it is to be inserted more than once, the element is cloned. These methods all return the jQuery object on which they are called. Note, however, that after `replaceWith()` runs, the elements in the jQuery object are no longer in the document:

```
// Add content at end of the #log element
$("#log").append("<br/>"+message);
// Add section sign at start of each <h1>
$("h1").prepend("§");
// Insert a rule before and after each <h1>
$("h1").before("<hr/>");
$("h1").after("<hr/>");
// Replace <hr/> tags with <br/> tags
$("hr").replaceWith("<br/>");
// Replace <h2> with <h1>, keeping content
$("h2").each(function() {
    var h2 = $(this);
    h2.replaceWith("<h1>" + h2.html() + "</h1>");
});
// after() and before() can also be called on text nodes.
// Here is another way to add § at the start of each <h1>
$("h1").map(function() {    // Map each <h1> element to
    return this.firstChild; // its first content node
}).before("§");
```

Each of these five structure-altering methods can also be passed a function that will be invoked to compute the value to be inserted. As usual, if you supply such a function it will be invoked once for each selected element. The this value will be that element, and the first argument will be the index of that element within the jQuery object. For the methods append(), prepend(), and replaceWith(), the second argument is the current content of the element as an HTML string. For before() and after(), the function is invoked with no second argument.

The five methods demonstrated above are all invoked on target elements and are passed the content that is to be inserted as an argument. Each of those five methods can be paired with another method that works the other way around: invoked on the content and passed the target elements as the argument. This table shows the method pairs:

Operation	$(target) .*method*(content)	$(content) .*method*(target)
insert content at end of target	append()	appendTo()
insert content at start of target	prepend()	prependTo()
insert content after target	after()	insertAfter()
insert content before target	before()	insertBefore()
replace target with content	replaceWith()	replaceAll()

The methods demonstrated in the example code above are in the second column; the methods in the third column are demonstrated below. But first there are a few important things to understand about these pairs of methods:

- If you pass a string to one of the methods in column two, it is taken as a string of HTML to insert. If you pass a string to one of the methods in column three, it is taken as a selector that identifies the target elements. (You can also identify the target elements directly by passing a jQuery object, Element, or text node.)

- The column three methods do not accept function arguments like the column two methods do.

- The methods in column two return the jQuery object on which they were invoked. The elements in that jQuery object may have new content or new siblings, but they are not themselves altered. The methods in column three are invoked on the content that is being inserted, and they return a new jQuery object that represents the new content after its insertion. In particular, note that if content is inserted at multiple locations, the returned jQuery object will include one element for each location.

With those differences listed, the code below performs the same operations as the code above, using the methods in the third column instead of the methods in the second column. Notice that in the second line we can't pass plain text (without angle brackets to identify it as HTML) to the $() method—it thinks we're specifying a selector. For this reason, we must explicitly create the text node that we want to insert:

```
// Append html to #log
$("<br/>+message").appendTo("#log");
// Append text node to <h1>s
$(document.createTextNode("§")).prependTo("h1");
// Insert rule before and after <h1>s
$("<hr/>").insertBefore("h1");
$("<hr/>").insertAfter("h1");
// Replace <hr/> with <br/>
$("<br/>").replaceAll("hr");
```

Copying Elements

As noted above, if you insert elements that are already part of the document, those elements will simply be moved, not copied, to their new location. If you are inserting the elements in more than one place, jQuery will make copies as needed, but copies are not made for only one insertion. If you want to copy elements to a new location instead of moving them, you must first make a copy with the clone() method. clone() makes and returns a copy of each selected element (and of all descendants of those elements). The elements in the returned jQuery object are not part of the document yet, but you can insert them with one of the methods above:

```
// Append a new div, with id "linklist" to the document
$(document.body)
    .append("<div id='linklist'><h1>Links</h1></div>");
// Copy all links in the document into that new div
$("a").clone().appendTo("#linklist");
// Add a <br/> after each link so they don't run together
$("#linklist > a").after("<br/>");
```

clone() does not normally copy event handlers (see Chapter 4) or other data you have associated with elements (see "Getting and Setting Element Data" on page 22); pass true if you want to clone that additional data as well.

Wrapping Elements

Another type of insertion into an HTML document involves wrapping a new element around one or more elements. jQuery defines three wrapping functions: `wrap()` wraps each of the selected elements, `wrapInner()` wraps the contents of each selected element, and `wrapAll()` wraps the selected elements as a group. These methods are usually passed a newly created wrapper element or a string of HTML used to create a wrapper. The HTML string can include multiple nested tags, if desired, but there must be a single innermost element. If you pass a function to any of these methods, it will be invoked once in the context of each element (with the element index as its only argument) and should return the wrapper string, Element, or jQuery object. Here are some examples:

```
// Wrap all <h1> tags with <i> tags
// Produces <i><h1>...</h1></i>
$("h1").wrap(document.createElement("i"));
// Wrap the content of all <h1> tags.
// Produces <h1><i>...</i></h1>
$("h1").wrapInner("<i/>");
// Wrap the first paragraph in an anchor and div
$("body>p:first")
    .wrap("<a name='f'><div class='first'></div></a>");
// Wrap all the other paragraphs in another div
$("body>p:not(:first)")
    .wrapAll("<div class='rest'></div>");
```

Deleting Elements

Along with insertions and replacements, jQuery also defines methods for deleting elements. `empty()` removes all children (including text nodes) of each of the selected elements without altering the elements themselves. The `remove()` method, by contrast, removes the selected elements (and all of their content) from the document. `remove()` is normally invoked with no arguments and removes all elements in the jQuery object. If you pass an argument, however, it is treated as a selector, and only elements of the jQuery object that also match the selector are removed. (If you just want to remove elements from the set of selected elements, without removing them from the document, use the `filter()` method, which is covered in "Selection Methods" on page 95.) Note that it is not necessary to remove elements before reinserting them into the document: you can simply insert them at a new location and they will be moved.

The `remove()` method removes any event handlers (see Chapter 4) and other data (see "Getting and Setting Element Data" on page 22) you may have bound to the removed elements. The `detach()` method works just like `remove()` but does not remove event handlers and data. `detach()` may be more useful when you want to temporarily remove elements from the document for later reinsertion.

Finally, the `unwrap()` method performs element removal in a way that is opposite of the `wrap()` or `wrapAll()` method: it removes the parent of each selected element without affecting the selected elements or their siblings. That is, for each selected element, it replaces the parent of that element with its children. Unlike `remove()` and `detach()`, `unwrap()` does not accept an optional selector argument.

CHAPTER 4

Events

One of the difficulties of working with events in client-side JavaScript is that IE (until IE9) implements a different event API than all other browsers. To address this difficulty, jQuery defines a uniform event API that works in all browsers. In its simple form, the jQuery API is easier to use than the standard or IE event APIs. And in its more complex full-featured form, the jQuery API is more powerful than the standard API. The sections below have all the details.

Simple Event Handler Registration

jQuery defines simple event registration methods for each of the commonly used and universally implemented browser events. To register an event handler for "click" events, for example, just call the click() method:

```
// Clicking on any <p> gives it a gray background
$("p").click(function() {
    $(this).css("background-color", "gray");
});
```

Calling a jQuery event registration method registers your handler on all of the selected elements. This is typically much easier than one-at-a-time event handler registration with addEventListener() or attachEvent().

These are the simple event handler registration methods jQuery defines:

blur()	focusin()	mousedown()	mouseup()
change()	focusout()	mouseenter()	resize()
click()	keydown()	mouseleave()	scroll()
dblclick()	keypress()	mousemove()	select()
error()	keyup()	mouseout()	submit()
focus()	load()	mouseover()	unload()

Most of these registration methods are for common event types with which you are probably already familiar. A few notes are in order, however. "focus" and "blur" events do not bubble, but the "focusin" and "focusout" events do, and jQuery ensures that these events work in all browsers. Conversely, the "mouseover" and "mouseout" events do bubble, which is often inconvenient because it is difficult to know whether the mouse has left the element you're interested in, or whether it has simply moved out of one of the descendants of that element. "mouseenter" and "mouseleave" are nonbubbling events that solve this problem. These event types were originally introduced by IE, and jQuery ensures that they work correctly in all browsers.

The "resize" and "unload" event types are only ever fired on the Window object, so if you want to register handlers for these event types, you should invoke the resize() and unload() methods on $(window). The scroll() method is also most often used on $(window), but it can also be used on any element that has scrollbars (such as when the CSS overflow attribute is set to "scroll" or "auto"). The load() method can be called on $(window) to register a "load" handler for the window, but it is usually better to pass your initialization function directly to $(), as shown in "The jQuery() Function" on page 4. You can use the load() method on iframes and images, however. Note that when invoked with different arguments, load() is also used to load new content (via scripted HTTP) into an element—see "The load() Method" on page 63. The error() method can be used on <img> elements to register handlers that are invoked if an image fails to load. It should not be used to set the Window onerror property.

In addition to these simple event registration methods, there are two special forms that are sometimes useful. The hover() method registers handlers for "mouseenter" and "mouseleave" events. Calling hover(f,g) is like calling mouseenter(f) and then calling mouseleave(g). If you pass just one argument to hover(), that function is used as the handler for both enter and leave events.

The other special event registration method is toggle(). This method binds event handler functions to the "click" event. You specify two or more handler functions and jQuery invokes one of them each time a click event occurs. If you call toggle(f,g,h), for example, the function f() is invoked to handle the first click event, g() is invoked to handle the second, h() is invoked to handle the third, and f() is invoked again to handle the fourth click event. Be careful when using toggle(): as we'll see in "Simple Effects" on page 52, this method can also be used to show or hide (i.e., toggle the visibility of) the selected elements.

We'll learn about other more general ways to register event handlers in the section "Advanced Event Handler Registration" on page 37, and we'll end this section with one more simple and convenient way to register handlers. Recall that you can pass a string of HTML to $() to create the elements described by that string, and that you can pass (as a second argument) an object of attributes to be set on the newly created elements. This second argument can be any object that you would pass to the attr() method. But, if any of the properties have the same name as the event registration methods listed above, the property value is taken as a handler function and is registered as a handler for the named event type. For example:

```
$("<img/>", {
    src: image_url,
    alt: image_description,
    className: "translucent_image",
    click: function() { $(this).css("opacity", "50%"); }
});
```

jQuery Event Handlers

The event handler functions in the examples above expect no arguments and return no values. It is quite normal to write event handlers like that, but jQuery does invoke every event handler with one or more arguments, and it does pay attention to the return value of your handlers. The most important thing you should know is that every event handler is passed a jQuery event object as its first argument. The fields of this object provide details (like mouse pointer coordinates) about the event. jQuery simulates the W3C standard Event object, even in browsers that do not support it (like IE8 and before), and jQuery event objects have the same set of fields in all browsers. This is explained in detail in "The jQuery Event Object" on page 34.

Normally, event handlers are invoked with only the single event object argument. But if you explicitly trigger an event with `trigger()` (see "Triggering Events" on page 41), you can pass an array of extra arguments. If you do this, those arguments will be passed to the event handler after the first event object argument.

Regardless of how they are registered, the return value of a jQuery event handler function is always significant. If a handler returns `false`, both the default action associated with the event and any future propagation of the event are canceled. That is, returning `false` is the same as calling the `preventDefault()` and `stopPropagation()` methods of the Event object. Also, when an event handler returns a value (other than `undefined`), jQuery stores that value in the `result` property of the Event object where it can be accessed by subsequently invoked event handlers.

The jQuery Event Object

jQuery hides implementation differences among browsers by defining its own Event object. When a jQuery event handler is invoked, it is always passed a jQuery Event object as its first argument. The jQuery Event object is based heavily on W3C standards, but it also codifies some de-facto event standards. jQuery does not define a hierarchy of Event object types, for example, there are not separate Event, MouseEvent, and Key-Event types. jQuery copies all of the following fields from the native Event object into every jQuery Event object (though some of them will be undefined for certain event types):

altKey	ctrlKey	newValue	screenX
attrChange	currentTarget	offsetX	screenY
attrName	detail	offsetY	shiftKey
bubbles	eventPhase	originalTarget	srcElement
button	fromElement	pageX	target
cancelable	keyCode	pageY	toElement
charCode	layerX	prevValue	view
clientX	layerY	relatedNode	wheelDelta
clientY	metaKey	relatedTarget	which

In addition to these properties, the Event object also defines the following methods:

```
preventDefault()           isDefaultPrevented()
stopPropagation()          isPropagationStopped()
stopImmediatePropagation() isImmediatePropagationStopped()
```

Most of these event properties and methods are standardized by the W3C, and you can read about them in any JavaScript reference. Some of these fields, shown in the following list, are specially handled by jQuery to give them a uniform cross-browser behavior:

metaKey

> If the native event object does not have a metaKey property, jQuery sets this to the same value as the ctrlKey property. In MacOS, the Command key sets the metaKey property.

pageX, pageY

> If the native event object does not define these properties but does define the viewport coordinates of the mouse pointer in clientX and clientY, jQuery computes the document coordinates of the mouse pointer and stores them in pageX and pageY.

target, currentTarget, relatedTarget

The target property is the document element on which the event occurred. If the native event object has a text node as the target, jQuery reports the containing Element instead. currentTarget is the element on which the current executing event handler was registered. This should always be the same as this.

If currentTarget is not the same as target, you're handling an event that has bubbled up from the element on which it occurred, and it may be useful to test the target element with the is() method (see "Queries and Query Results" on page 8):

```
// Ignore events that start on links
if ($(event.target).is("a")) return;
```

relatedTarget is the other element involved in transition events such as "mouseover" and "mouseout". For "mouseover" events, for example, the relatedTarget property specifies the element that the mouse pointer exited as it moved over the target. If the native event object does not define relatedTarget but does define toElement and fromElement, relatedTarget is set from those properties.

timeStamp

The time at which the event occurred, in the millisecond representation returned by the Date.getTime() method. jQuery sets the field itself to work around a long-standing bug in Firefox.

which

jQuery normalizes this nonstandard event property so that it specifies which mouse button or keyboard key was pressed during the event. For keyboard events, if the native event does not define which but defines charCode or keyCode, then which will be set to whichever of those properties is defined. For mouse events, if which is not defined but the button property is defined, which is set based on the button value: 0 means no buttons are pressed, 1 means the left button is pressed, 2 means the middle button is pressed, and 3 means the right button is pressed. (Note that some browsers don't generate mouse events for right-button clicks.)

In addition, the following fields of the jQuery Event object are jQuery-specific additions that you may sometimes find useful:

data

> If additional data was specified when the event handler was registered (see "Advanced Event Handler Registration"), it is made available to the handler as the value of this field.

handler

> A reference to the event handler function currently being invoked.

result

> The return value of the most recently invoked handler for this event, ignoring handlers that do not return a value.

originalEvent

> A reference to the native Event object generated by the browser.

Advanced Event Handler Registration

We've seen that jQuery defines quite a few simple methods for registering event handlers. Each of these simply invokes the single, more complex method bind() to bind a handler for a named event type to each of the elements in the jQuery object. Using bind() directly allows you to use advanced event registration features that are not available through the simpler methods.*

---

* jQuery uses the term "bind" for event handler registration. ECMAScript 5, and a number of JavaScript frameworks, define a bind() method on functions, and use the term for the association of functions with objects on which they are to be invoked. jQuery's version of the Function.bind() method is a utility function named jQuery.proxy(), which you can read about in Chapter 7.

In its simplest form, **bind()** expects an event type string as its first argument and an event handler function as its second. The simple event registration methods use this form of **bind()**. The call **$('p').click(f)**, for example, is equivalent to:

```
$('p').bind('click', f);
```

bind() can also be invoked with three arguments. In this form, the event type is the first argument and the handler function is the third. You can pass any value between those two and jQuery will set the **data** property of the Event object to the value you specify before it invokes the handler. It is sometimes useful to pass additional data to your handlers in this way without having to use closures.

There are other advanced features of **bind()** as well. If the first argument is a space-separated list of event types, the handler function will be registered for each of the named event types. The call **$('a').hover(f)** (see "Simple Event Handler Registration" on page 31), for example, is the same as:

```
$('a').bind('mouseenter mouseleave', f);
```

Another important feature of **bind()** is that it allows you to specify a namespace (or namespaces) for your event handlers when you register them. This allows you to define groups of handlers, which comes in handy if you later want to trigger or de-register the handlers in a particular namespace. Handler namespaces are especially useful for programmers who are writing libraries or modules of reusable jQuery code. Event namespaces look like CSS class selectors. To bind an event handler in a namespace, add a period and the namespace name to the event type string:

```
// Bind f as a mouseover handler in namespace "myMod"
$('a').bind('mouseover.myMod', f);
```

You can even assign a handler to multiple namespaces, like this:

```
// Bind f as a mouseout handler in two namespaces
$('a').bind('mouseout.myMod.yourMod', f);
```

The final feature of bind() is that the first argument can be an object that maps event names to handler functions. To reuse the hover() method example, the call $('a').hover(f,g) is the same as:

```
$('a').bind({mouseenter:f, mouseleave:g});
```

When you use this form of bind(), the property names in the object you pass can be space-separated strings of event types and can include namespaces. If you specify a second argument after the first object argument, that value is used as the data argument for each of the event bindings.

jQuery has another event handler registration method: one(). This method is invoked and works just like bind(), except that the event handler you register will automatically de-register itself after it is invoked. As the method name implies, this means that event handlers registered with one() will never be triggered more than once.

One feature that bind() and one() do not have is the ability to register capturing event handlers as you can with addEventListener(). IE (until IE9) does not support capturing handlers, and jQuery does not attempt to simulate that feature.

Deregistering Event Handlers

After registering an event handler with bind() (or with any of the simpler event registration methods) you can deregister it with unbind() to prevent it from being triggered by future events. (Note that unbind() only deregisters event handlers registered with bind() and related jQuery methods. It does not deregister handlers passed to addEventListener() or the IE method attachEvent(), and it does not remove handlers defined by element attributes such as onclick and onmouseover.) With no arguments, unbind() deregisters all event handlers (for all event types) for all elements in the jQuery object:

```
// Remove all jQuery event handlers from all elements!
$('*').unbind();
```

With one string argument, all handlers for the named event type (or types, if the string names more than one) are unbound from all elements in the jQuery object:

```
// Unbind all mouseover and mouseout handlers
// of all <a> tags
$('a').unbind("mouseover mouseout");
```

This is a heavy-handed approach and should not be used in modular code because someone might also be using other modules that register their own handlers for the same event types on the same elements. If your module registered event handlers using namespaces, however, you can use this one-argument version of **unbind()** to deregister only the handlers in your namespace:

```
// Unbind all mouseover and mouseout handlers
// in the "myMod" namespace
$('a').unbind("mouseover.myMod mouseout.myMod");
// Unbind handlers for any event in the myMod namespace
$('a').unbind(".myMod");
// Unbind click handlers that are in both namespaces
$('a').unbind("click.ns1.ns2");
```

If you want to be careful to unbind only event handlers you registered yourself, and you did not use namespaces, you must retain a reference to the event handler functions and use the two-argument version of **unbind()**. In this form, the first argument is an event type string (without namespaces), and the second argument is a handler function:

```
$('#mybutton').unbind('click', myClickHandler);
```

When invoked this way, **unbind()** deregisters the specified event handler function for events of the specified type (or types) from all elements in the jQuery object. Note that event handlers can be unbound using this two-argument version of **unbind()**, even when they were registered with an extra data value using the three-argument version of **bind()**.

You can also pass a single object argument to **unbind()**. In this case, **unbind()** is invoked recursively for each property of the object. The property name is used as the event type string, and the property value is used as the handler function:

```
$('a').unbind({  // Remove specific event handlers
    mouseover: mouseoverHandler,
    mouseout: mouseoutHandler
});
```

Finally, there is one more way that **unbind()** can be invoked. If you pass a jQuery Event object to it, it unbinds the event handler to which that event was passed. Calling **unbind(ev)** is equivalent to **unbind(ev.type, ev.handler)**.

Triggering Events

The event handlers you register are automatically invoked when the user uses the mouse or keyboard, or when other kinds of events occur. Sometimes, however, it is useful to be able to trigger events manually. The simple way to do this is to invoke one of the event registration methods (like **click()** or **mouse over()**) with no argument. Just as many jQuery methods serve as both getters and setters, these event methods register an event handler when invoked with an argument, and trigger event handlers when invoked with no arguments. For example:

```
// Act as if the user clicked the Submit button
$("#my_form").submit();
```

The **submit()** method in the line above synthesizes an Event object and triggers any event handlers that have been registered for the "submit" event. If none of those event handlers returns **false** or calls the **preventDefault()** method of the Event object, the form will actually be submitted. Note that events that bubble will do so even when triggered manually. This means that triggering an event on a selected set of elements may also trigger handlers on the ancestors of those elements.

It is important to note that jQuery's event triggering methods will trigger any handlers registered with jQuery's event registration methods, and they will also trigger handlers defined on HTML attributes or Element properties such as **onsubmit**. But you cannot manually trigger event handlers registered with **addEventListener()** or **attachEvent()** (those handlers will still be invoked when a real event occurs, however).

It is also important to note that jQuery's event triggering mechanism is synchronous—there is no event queue involved. When you trigger an event, event handlers are invoked immediately, before the triggering method you called returns. If you trigger a "click" event, and one of the triggered handlers triggers a "submit" event, all of the matching submit handlers are invoked before the next "click" handler is invoked.

Methods like submit() are convenient for binding and triggering events, but just as jQuery defines a more general bind() method, it also defines a more general trigger() method. Normally, you invoke trigger() with an event type string as the first argument, and it triggers the handlers registered for events of that type on all elements in the jQuery object. So, the submit() call above is equivalent to:

```
$("#my_form").trigger("submit");
```

Unlike the bind() and unbind() methods, you cannot specify more than one event type in this string. Like bind() and unbind(), however, you can specify event namespaces to trigger only the handlers defined in that namespace. If you want to trigger only event handlers that have *no* namespace, append an exclamation mark to the event type. Handlers registered through properties like onclick are considered to have no namespace:

```
// Trigger button click handlers in namespace ns1
$("button").trigger("click.ns1");
// Trigger button click handlers in no namespace
$("button").trigger("click!");
```

Instead of passing an event type string as the first argument to trigger(), you can also pass an Event object (or any object that has a type property). The type property will be used to determine what kind of handlers to trigger. If you specified a jQuery Event object, it will be the one passed to the triggered handlers. If you specified a plain object, a new jQuery Event object will be created, and the properties of the object you passed will be added to it. This is an easy way to pass additional data to event handlers:

```
// The onclick handler of button1 triggers
// the same event on button2
$('#button1').click(function(e) {
    $('#button2').trigger(e);
});

// Add extra property to the event object when triggering
$('#button1').trigger({type:'click', synthetic:true});

// Test extra property to distinguish real from synthetic
$('#button1').click(function(e) {
    if (e.synthetic) {...};
});
```

There is another way to pass additional data to event handlers when you trigger them manually. The value you pass as the second argument to **trigger()** will become the second argument to each of the event handlers that is triggered. If you pass an array as the second argument, each of its elements will be passed as arguments to the triggered handlers:

```
// Pass a single extra argument
$('#button1').trigger("click", true);
// Pass three extra arguments
$('#button1').trigger("click", [x,y,z]);
```

Sometimes you may want to trigger all handlers for a given event type, regardless of which document element those handlers are bound to. You could select all elements with $('*') and then call **trigger()** on the result, but that would be very inefficient. Instead, call the jQuery.event.trigger() utility function, which takes the same arguments as the **trigger()** method but efficiently triggers event handlers for the specified event type throughout the document. Note that "global events" triggered in this way do not bubble, and only handlers registered using jQuery methods (not event handlers registered with DOM properties like **onclick**) are triggered with this technique.

After invoking event handlers, **trigger()** (and the convenience methods that call it) perform whatever default action is associated with the triggered event (assuming that the event handlers didn't return false or call **preventDefault()** on the event object). For example, if you trigger a "submit" event on a `<form>` element, `trigger()` will call the `submit()` method of that form, and if you trigger a "focus" event on an element, `trigger()` will call the `focus()` method of that element.

If you want to invoke event handlers without performing the default action, use `triggerHandler()`, which works just like `trigger()` except that it first calls the `preventDefault()` and `cancelBubble()` methods of the Event object. This means that the synthetic event does not bubble or perform the default action associated with it.

Custom Events

jQuery's event management system is designed around the standard events like mouse clicks and key presses that web browsers generate. But it is not tied to those events, and you can use any string you want as an event type name. With `bind()`, you can register handlers for this kind of "custom event", and with `trigger()` you can cause those handlers to be invoked.

This kind of indirect invocation of custom event handlers turns out to be quite useful for writing modular code and implementing a publish/subscribe model or the Observer pattern. When using custom events you may find it useful to trigger them globally with the `jQuery.event.trigger()` function instead of the `trigger()` method:

```
// When the user clicks the "logoff" button, broadcast a
// custom event to any interested observers that need to
// save their state and then navigate to the logoff page.
$("#logoff").click(function() {
    $.event.trigger("logoff");     // Broadcast an event
    window.location = "logoff.php"; // Go to a new page
});
```

We'll see in "Ajax Events" on page 80 that jQuery's Ajax methods broadcast custom events like this to notify interested listeners.

Live Events

The `bind()` method binds event handlers to specific document elements, just as `addEventListener()` and `attachEvent()` do. But web applications that use jQuery often dynamically create new elements. If we've used `bind()` to bind an event handler to all `<a>` elements in the document, and then we create new document content with new `<a>` elements, those new elements will not have the same event handlers as the old ones, so they will behave differently.

jQuery addresses this issue with "live events". To use live events, use the `delegate()` and `undelegate()` methods instead of `bind()` and `unbind()`. `delegate()` is usually invoked on `$(document)` and is passed a jQuery selector string, a jQuery event type string, and a jQuery event handler function. It registers an internal handler on the document or window (or on whatever elements are in the jQuery object). When an event of the specified type bubbles up to this internal handler, it determines whether the target of the event (the element that the event occurred on) matches the selector string. If so, it invokes the specified handler function. So to handle "mouseover" events on both old and newly created `<a>` elements, you might register a handler like this:

```
$(document).delegate("a", "mouseover", linkHandler);
```

Or, you might use `bind()` in the static portions of your document and then use `delegate()` to handle the portions that change dynamically:

```
// Static event handlers for static links
$("a").bind("mouseover", linkHandler);
// Live event handlers for dynamic parts of the document
$(".dynamic").delegate("a", "mouseover", linkHandler);
```

Just as the `bind()` method has a three-argument version that allows you to specify the value of the `data` property of the event object, the `delegate()` method has a four-argument version that allows the same thing. To use this version, pass the data value as the third argument and the handler function as the fourth.

It is important to understand that live events depend on event bubbling. By the time an event bubbles up to the document object, it may have already been passed to a number of static event handlers. And if any of those handlers called the `cancel Bubble()` method of the Event object, the live event handler will never be invoked.

jQuery defines a method named `live()` that can also be used to register live events. `live()` is a little harder to understand than `delegate()`, but it has the same two- or three-argument signature as `bind()` and is more commonly used. The two calls to `delegate()` shown above could also be written using `live()`:

```
$("a").live("mouseover", linkHandler);
$("a", $(".dynamic")).live("mouseover", linkHandler);
```

When the `live()` method is invoked on a jQuery object, the elements in that object are not actually used. What matters instead is the selector string and the context object (the first and second arguments to `$()`) that were used to create the jQuery object. jQuery objects make these values available through their `context` and `selector` properties (see "Queries and Query Results" on page 8). Normally, you invoke `$()` with only one argument and the context is the current document. So for a jQuery object `x`, the following two lines of code do the same thing:

```
x.live(type,handler);
$(x.context).delegate(x.selector, type, handler);
```

To deregister live event handlers, use `die()` or `undelegate()`. `die()` can be invoked with one or two arguments. With one event type argument, it removes all live event handlers that match the selector and the event type. And with an event type and handler function argument, it removes only the one specified handler. Some examples:

```
// Remove all live handlers for mouseover on <a> tags
$('a').die('mouseover');
```

```
// Remove just one specific live handler
$('a').die('mouseover', linkHandler);
```

undelegate() is like **die()** but more explicitly separates the context (the elements on which the internal event handlers are registered) and the selector string. The calls to **die()** above could instead be written like this:

```
// Remove all live handlers for <a> tags
$(document).undelegate('a');
// Remove all live mouseover handlers for <a> tags
$(document).undelegate('a', 'mouseover');
// Remove one live mouseover handler for <a> tags
$(document).undelegate('a', 'mouseover', linkHandler);
```

Finally, **undelegate()** can also be called with no arguments at all. In this case, it deregisters all live event handlers that are delegated from the selected elements.

CHAPTER 5

Animated Effects

One powerful feature of client-side JavaScript is that you can script the CSS styles of document elements. By setting the CSS `visibility` property, for example, you can make elements appear and disappear. With clever programming, you can even produce animated visual effects. Instead of just making an element disappear, for example, you might reduce the value of its `opacity` property over the period of a half-second so that it quickly fades away instead of just blinking out of existence. This kind of animated visual effect creates a more pleasing experience for users, and jQuery makes them easy.

jQuery defines simple methods such as `fadeIn()` and `fade Out()` for basic visual effects. In addition to simple effects methods, it defines an `animate()` method for producing more complex custom animations. The sections below explain both the simple effects methods and the more general `animate()` method. First, however, we'll describe some general features of jQuery's animation framework.

For every animation, you need to specify a duration of time—in milliseconds or by using a string—for how long the effect should last. The string "fast" means 200ms. The string "slow" means 600ms. If you specify a duration string that jQuery does not recognize, or if you omit it, you'll get a default duration of 400ms. You can define new duration names by adding new string-to-number mappings to `jQuery.fx.speeds`:

```
jQuery.fx.speeds["medium-fast"] = 300;
jQuery.fx.speeds["medium-slow"] = 500;
```

jQuery's effects methods usually take the effect duration as an optional first argument. Some methods, however, produce an instant nonanimated effect when you omit the duration:

```
$("#message").fadeIn();          // Fade in over 400ms
$("#message").fadeOut("fast");   // Fade out over 200ms
$("#message").show();            // Show instantly
```

Disabling Animations

Animated visual effects have become the norm on many websites, but not all users like them—some find them distracting, and others feel they cause motion sickness. Disabled users may find that animations interfere with assistive technology like screen readers, and users on old hardware may feel that such effects require too much processing power. As a courtesy to your users, you should generally keep your animations simple and understated, and also provide an option to disable them completely. jQuery makes it easy to disable all effects globally: simply set jQuery.fx.off to true. This has the effect of changing the duration of every animation to 0ms, making them behave as instantaneous, nonanimated changes.

To allow end-users to disable effects, you might use code like this in your scripts:

```
$(".stopmoving").click(function() {
    jQuery.fx.off = true;
});
```

Then, if the web designer includes an element with class "stopmoving" on the page, the user can click it to disable animations.

---

jQuery's effects are asynchronous. When you call an animation method like fadeIn(), it returns right away and the animation is performed "in the background". Because animation methods return before the animation is complete, the second argument (also optional) to many of jQuery's effects methods is a function that will be invoked when the effect is complete. The function is not passed any arguments, but the `this` value is set to the document element that was animated. The callback function is invoked once for each selected element:

```
// Quickly fade in an element, and when it is visible,
// display some text in it.
$("#message").fadeIn("fast", function() {
    $(this).text("Hello World");
});
```

Passing a callback function to an effect method allows you to perform actions at the end of an effect. Note, however, that this is not necessary when you simply want to perform multiple effects in sequence. By default, jQuery's animations are queued ("The Animation Options Object" on page 55 shows how to override this default). If you call an animation method on an element that is already being animated, the new animation does not begin right away but is deferred until the current animation ends. For example, you can make an element blink before fading in permanently:

```
$("#blinker").fadeIn(100).fadeOut(100)
             .fadeIn(100).fadeOut(100)
             .fadeIn();
```

jQuery's effects methods are declared to accept optional duration and callback arguments. It is also possible to invoke these methods with an object whose properties specify animation options:

```
// Pass duration and callback as object properties
$("#message").fadeIn({
    duration: "fast",
    complete: function(){ $(this).text("Hello World"); }
});
```

Passing an object of animation objects is most commonly done with the general `animate()` method, but it is also possible for the simpler effects methods. Using an options object allows you to set other advanced options to control queuing and easing, for example. The available options are explained in "The Animation Options Object" on page 55.

Simple Effects

jQuery defines nine simple effects methods to hide and show elements. They can be divided into three groups based on the kind of effect they perform:

fadeIn(), fadeOut(), fadeTo()

> These are the simplest effects: fadeIn() and fadeOut() animate the CSS opacity property to show or hide an element. Both accept optional duration and callback arguments. fadeTo() is slightly different: it expects a target opacity argument and animates the change from the element's current opacity to this target. For the fadeTo() method, the duration (or options object) is required as the first argument, and the target opacity is required as the second argument. The callback function is an optional third argument.

show(), hide(), toggle()

> The fadeOut() method listed above makes elements invisible but retains space for them in the document layout. The hide() method, by contrast, removes the elements from the layout as if the CSS display property was set to none. When invoked with no arguments, hide() and show() simply hide or show the selected elements immediately. With a duration (or options object) argument, however, they animate the hiding or showing process. hide() shrinks an element's width and height to 0 at the same time that it reduces the element's opacity to 0. show() reverses the process.

> toggle() changes the visibility state of the elements it is invoked on: if they are hidden, it calls show(); if they are visible, it calls hide(). As with show() and hide(), you must pass a duration or options object to toggle() to get an animated effect. Passing true to toggle() is the same as calling show() with no arguments, and passing false() is the same as calling hide() with no arguments. Note also that if you pass two or more function arguments

to `toggle()`, it registers event handlers, as described in "Simple Event Handler Registration" on page 31.

`slideDown()`, `slideUp()`, `slideToggle()`

`slideUp()` hides the elements in the jQuery object by animating their height to 0 and then setting the CSS `display` property to "none". `slideDown()` reverses the process to make a hidden element visible again. `slideToggle()` toggles the visibility of an item using a slide up or slide down animation. Each of the three methods accepts the optional duration and callback arguments (or the options object argument).

Here is an example that invokes methods from each of these groups. Keep in mind that jQuery's animations are queued by default, so these animations are performed one after the other:

```
// Fade out, then show, then slide up, then slide down
$("img").fadeOut().show(300).slideUp().slideToggle();
```

Various jQuery plugins (see Chapter 9) add additional effect methods to the library. The jQuery UI library (see Chapter 10) includes a particularly comprehensive set of effects.

Custom Animations

You can use the `animate()` method to produce more general animated effects than are available with the simple effects methods. The first argument to `animate()` specifies what to animate, and the remaining arguments specify how to animate it. The first argument is required: it must be an object whose properties specify CSS attributes and their target values. `animate()` animates the CSS properties of each element from its current value to the specified target value. So, for example, the `slideUp()` effect described above can also be performed with code like this:

```
// Shrink the height of all images to 0
$("img").animate({ height: 0 });
```

As an optional second argument, you can pass an options object to `animate()`:

```
$("#sprite").animate({
    opacity: .25,        // Animate opacity to .25
    font-size: 10        // Animate font size to 10 pixels
}, {
    duration: 500,       // Animation lasts 1/2 second
    complete: function() {   // Call this when done
        this.text("Goodbye"); // Change element text.
    }
});
```

Instead of passing an options object as the second argument, `animate()` also allows you to specify three of the most commonly used options as arguments. You can pass the duration (as a number or string) as the second argument. You can specify the name of an easing function (which will be explained shortly) as the third argument. And you can specify a callback function as the fourth argument.

In the most general case, `animate()` accepts two object arguments: the first specifies what to animate, and the second specifies how to animate it. To fully understand how to perform animations with jQuery, there are additional details about both objects that you must know.

The Animation Properties Object

The first argument to `animate()` must be an object. The property names for this object must be CSS attribute names, and the values of those properties must be the target values toward which the animation will move. Only numeric properties can be animated: it is not possible to animate colors, fonts, or enumerated properties such as `display`. If the value of a property is a number, pixels are assumed. If the value is a string, you may specify units. If you omit the units, pixels are again assumed. To specify relative values, prefix the value string with "+=" to increase the value or with "-=" to decrease the value. For example:

```
$("p").animate({
    "margin-left": "+=.5in", // Increase indent
    opacity: "-=.1"          // And decrease opacity
});
```

Note the use of the quotes around the property name "margin-left" in the object literal above. The hyphen in this property name means that it is not a legal JavaScript identifier, so it must be quoted here. jQuery also allows you to use the mixed-case alternative "marginLeft", of course.

In addition to numeric values (with optional units and "+=" and "-=" prefixes), there are three other values that can be used in jQuery animation objects. The value "hide" will save the current state of the property and then animate that property toward 0. The value "show" will animate a CSS property toward its saved value. If an animation uses "show", jQuery will call the show() method when the animation completes. And if an animation uses "hide", jQuery will call hide() when the animation completes. You can also use the value "toggle" to perform either a show or a hide depending on the current setting of the attribute. You can produce a "slideRight" effect (similar to the slideUp() method, but animating element width) like this:

```
$("img").animate({
    width: "hide",
    borderLeft: "hide",
    borderRight: "hide",
    paddingLeft: "hide",
    paddingRight: "hide"
});
```

Replace the property values with "show" or "toggle" to produce sideways slide effects analogous to slideDown() and slideToggle().

The Animation Options Object

The second argument to animate() is an optional object that holds options specifying how the animation is performed. You've already seen two of the most important options. The duration property specifies the length of the animation in milliseconds, or as the string "fast", "slow", or any name you've defined in jQuery.fx.speeds.

Another option you've already seen is the complete property: it specifies a function that will be called when the animation is complete. A similar property, step, specifies a function that is called for each step or frame of the animation. The element being animated is the this value, and the current value of the property being animated is passed as the first argument.

The queue property of the options object specifies whether the animation should be queued, or whether it should be deferred until any pending animations have completed. By default, animations are queued, but you can disable this by setting the queue property to false. Unqueued animations start immediately. Subsequent queued animations are not deferred for unqueued animations. Consider the following code:

```
$("img").fadeIn(500)
        .animate({"width":"+=100"},
                 {queue:false, duration:1000})
        .fadeOut(500);
```

The fadeIn() and fadeOut() effects are queued, but the call to animate() (which animates the width property for 1000ms) is not queued. The width animation begins at the same time the fadeIn() effect begins. The fadeOut() effect begins as soon as the fadeIn() effect ends—it does not wait for the width animation to complete.

The remaining animation options involve easing functions. The easing property of the options object specifies the name of an easing function. By default, jQuery uses the sinusoidal function it calls "swing". If you want your animations to be linear, use an options object like this:

```
$("img").animate({"width":"+=100"},
                 {duration: 500, easing:"linear"});
```

Recall that the duration, easing, and complete options can also be specified by arguments to animate() instead of passing an options object. So, the animation above could also be written like this:

```
$("img").animate({"width":"+=100"}, 500, "linear");
```

Easing Functions

The straightforward but naïve way to perform animations involves a linear mapping between time and the value being animated. If we are 100ms into a 400ms animation, for example, the animation is 25% done. If we are animating the opacity property from 1.0 to 0.0 (for a fadeOut() call, perhaps), in a linear animation, the opacity should be at 0.75 at this point in the animation. It turns out, however, that visual effects are more pleasing if they are not linear. So, jQuery interposes an "easing function" that maps from a time-based completion percentage to the desired effect percentage. jQuery calls the easing function with a time-based value between 0 and 1. It returns another value between 0 and 1, and jQuery computes the value of the CSS property based on this computed value. Generally, easing functions are expected to return 0 when passed the value 0, and 1 when passed the value 1, of course. But they can be nonlinear between those two values, which makes the animation appear to accelerate and decelerate.

jQuery's default easing function is a sinusoid: it starts off slow, then speeds up, then slows down again to "ease" the animation to its final value. jQuery gives its easing functions names. The default is named "swing", and jQuery also implements a linear function named "linear". You can add your own easing functions to the jQuery.easing object:

```
jQuery.easing["squareroot"] = Math.sqrt;
```

The jQuery UI library and a plugin known simply as "the jQuery Easing Plugin" define a comprehensive set of additional easing functions.

Finally, jQuery's animation framework even allows you to specify different easing functions for the different CSS properties you want to animate. There are two different ways to achieve this, demonstrated by the code below:

```
// Hide images, as with the hide() method, but animate
// the image size linearly while the opacity is being
// animated with the default "swing" easing function.

// Use the specialEasing option
$("img").animate({
                  width:"hide",
                  height:"hide",
                  opacity:"hide"
                },{
                    specialEasing: {
                       width: "linear",
                       height: "linear"
                    }
                });

// Or pass [target value, easing function] arrays
$("img").animate({
    width: ["hide", "linear"],
    height: ["hide", "linear"],
    opacity:"hide"
});
```

Canceling, Delaying, and Queuing Effects

jQuery defines a few more animation and queue-related methods that you should know about. The stop() method is first:
it stops any currently executing animations on the selected elements. stop() accepts two optional boolean arguments. If the
first argument is true, the animation queue will be cleared for
the selected elements, canceling any pending animations as
well as stopping the current one. The default is false: if this
argument is omitted, queued animations are not canceled. The
second argument specifies whether the CSS properties being
animated should be left as they are currently, or whether they
should be set to their final target values. true sets them to their
final values; false (or omitting the argument) leaves them at
whatever their current value is.

When animations are triggered by user events, you may want
to cancel any current or queued animations before beginning
a new one. For example:

```
// Images become opaque when the mouse moves over them.
// But don't keep queueing up animations on mouse events!
$("img").bind({
    mouseover: function() {
        $(this).stop().fadeTo(300, 1.0);
    },
    mouseout: function() {
        $(this).stop().fadeTo(300, 0.5);
    }
});
```

The second animation-related method we'll cover here is delay(), which simply adds a timed delay to the animation queue. Pass a duration in milliseconds (or a duration string) as the first argument and a queue name as the optional second argument (the second argument is not normally needed—we'll talk about queue names below). You can use delay() in compound animations like this one:

```
// Quickly fade out halfway, wait, then slide up
$("img").fadeTo(100, 0.5).delay(200).slideUp();
```

In the stop() method example above, we used "mouseover" and "mouseout" events to animate the opacity of images. We can refine that example by adding a short delay before the animation begins. That way, if the mouse quickly moves through an image without stopping, no distracting animation occurs:

```
$("img").bind({
    mouseover: function() {
        $(this).stop(true).delay(100).fadeTo(300, 1.0);
    },
    mouseout: function() {
        $(this).stop(true).fadeTo(300, 0.5);
    }
});
```

The final animation-related methods are ones that give low-level access to the jQuery queuing mechanism. jQuery queues are lists of functions to be executed in sequence. Each queue is associated with a document element (or the Document or Window objects), and each element's queues are independent of other elements' queues. You can add a new function to the queue with the queue() method. When your function reaches the head of the queue, it will be automatically dequeued and invoked. When your function is invoked, the **this** value is the element with which it is associated. Your function will be passed a function as its single argument. When your function has completed its operation, it must invoke the function that was passed to it. This runs the next operation in the queue, and if you don't call the function, the queue will stall and queued functions will never get invoked.

We've seen that you can pass a callback function to jQuery's effects methods in order to perform some kind of action after the effect completes. You can achieve the same thing by queuing up your function:

```
// Fade in, wait, set some text, and animate the border
$("#message").fadeIn().delay(200).queue(function(next) {
    $(this).text("Hello  World"); // Display some text
    next();                       // Run next queued item
}).animate({borderWidth: "+=10px;"});  // Grow the border
```

The function argument to queued functions is a new feature in jQuery 1.4. In code written for earlier versions of the library, queued functions dequeue the next function "manually" by calling the **dequeue()** method:

```
$(this).dequeue();  // Instead of next()
```

If there is nothing in the queue, calling **dequeue()** does nothing. Otherwise, it removes a function from the head of the queue and invokes it, setting the **this** value and passing the function described above.

There are a few more heavy-handed ways to manipulate the queue. **clearQueue()** clears the queue. Passing an array of functions to **queue()** instead of a single function replaces the queue with the new array of functions. And calling **queue()** with neither a function nor an array of functions returns the current queue as an array. Also, jQuery defines versions of the **queue()** and **dequeue()** methods as utility functions. If you want to add the function **f** to the queue for an element **e**, you can use either the method or the function:

```
// Create a jQuery object holding e, and call queue()
$(e).queue(f);
// Just call the jQuery.queue() utility function
jQuery.queue(e,f);
```

Finally, note that queue(), dequeue(), and clearQueue() all take
an optional queue name as their first argument. jQuery's effects
and animation methods use a queue named "fx", which is the
queue that is used if you do not specify a queue name. jQuery's
queue mechanism is useful whenever you need to perform
asynchronous operations sequentially: instead of passing a
callback function to each asynchronous operation so that it can
trigger the next function in the sequence, you can use a queue
to manage the sequence instead. Simply pass a queue name
other than "fx", and remember that queued functions do not
execute automatically. You must explicitly call dequeue() to
run the first one, and each operation must dequeue the next
one when it finishes.

CHAPTER 6

Ajax

Ajax is the popular name for web application programming techniques that use HTTP scripting to load data, without causing page refreshes. Because Ajax techniques are so useful in modern web apps, jQuery includes Ajax utilities to simplify them. jQuery defines one high-level utility method and four high-level utility functions. These high-level utilities are all based on the powerful low-level function `jQuery.ajax()`. The subsections that follow describe the high-level utilities first, and then cover the `jQuery.ajax()` function in detail. In order to fully understand the operation of the high-level utilities, you'll need to understand `jQuery.ajax()`, even if you never need to use it explicitly.

The load() Method

The `load()` method is the simplest of all jQuery utilities: pass it a URL, which it will asynchronously load the content of, and then insert that content into each of the selected elements, replacing any content that is already there. For example:

```
// Load and display a status report every 60 seconds
setInterval(function() {
    $("#stats").load("status_report.html");
}, 60000);
```

We also saw the `load()` method in "Simple Event Handler Registration" on page 31 where it was used to register a handler for "load" events. If the first argument to this method is a function instead of a string, it behaves as an event handler registration method instead of as an Ajax method.

If you only want to display a portion of the loaded document, add a space to the URL and follow it with a jQuery selector. When the URL has loaded, the selector you specified will be used to select the portions of the loaded HTML to be displayed:

```
// Load the temperature section of the weather report
$('#temp').load("weather_report.html #temperature");
```

Note that the selector at the end of this URL looks very much like a fragment identifier. The space is required, however, if you want jQuery to insert only the selected portion (or portions) of the loaded document.

The `load()` method accepts two optional arguments in addition to the required URL. The first is data to append to the URL or to send along with the request. If you pass a string, it is appended to the URL (after a `?` or `&`, as needed). If you pass an object, it is converted to a string of ampersand-separated `name=value` pairs and sent along with the request. (The details of object-to-string conversion for Ajax are in "Passing Data to jQuery's Ajax Utilities" on page 68). The `load()` method normally makes an HTTP GET request, but if you pass a data object, it makes a POST request instead. Here are two examples:

```
// Load the weather report for a specified zipcode
$('#temp').load("us_weather.html", "zipcode=02134");

// Here we use an object as data and specify degrees F
$('#temp').load("us_weather.html",
                { zipcode:02134, units:'F' });
```

jQuery's Ajax Status Codes

All of jQuery's Ajax utilities, including the load() method, invoke callback functions to provide asynchronous notification of the success or failure of the request. The second argument to these callbacks is a string with one of the following values:

"success"

This indicates that the request completed successfully.

"notmodified"

This code indicates that the request completed normally but that the server sent an HTTP 304 "Not Modified" response, which means that the requested URL has not changed since it was last requested. This status code only occurs if you set the ifModified option to true (see "Common Options" on page 73). jQuery 1.4 considers a "notmodified" status code a success, but earlier versions consider it an error.

"error"

This indicates that the request did not complete successfully because of an HTTP error of some sort. For more details, you can check the HTTP status code in the XMLHttpRequest object, which is also passed to each callback.

"timeout"

If an Ajax request does not complete within the timeout interval that you select, the error callback is invoked with this status code. By default, jQuery Ajax requests do not time out; you'll only see this status code if you set the timeout option (see "Common Options" on page 73).

"parsererror"

This status code indicates that the HTTP request completed successfully but that jQuery could not parse it in the way it expected to. This status code occurs if the server sends a malformed XML document or malformed JSON text, for example. Note that this status code is "parsererror" not "parseerror".

Another optional argument to `load()` is a callback function that will be invoked when the Ajax request completes. If it's successful, it will be invoked after the URL has been loaded and inserted into the selected elements. If you don't specify any data, you can pass this callback function as the second argument. Otherwise, it should be the third argument. The callback you specify will be invoked once as a method of each of the elements in the jQuery object, and it will be passed three arguments to each invocation: the complete text of the loaded URL, a status code string, and the XMLHttpRequest object that was used to load the URL. The status argument is a jQuery status code, not an HTTP status code, and it will be a string like "success", "error", or "timeout".

Ajax Utility Functions

The other high-level jQuery Ajax utilities are functions, not methods, and they are invoked directly through `jQuery` or `$`, not on a jQuery object. `jQuery.getScript()` loads and executes files of JavaScript code. `jQuery.getJSON()` loads a URL, parses it as JSON, and passes the resulting object to the specified callback. Both of these functions call `jQuery.get()`, which is a more general purpose URL-fetching function. Finally, `jQuery.post()` works just like `jQuery.get()` but performs an HTTP POST request instead of a GET. Like the `load()` method, all of these functions are asynchronous: they return to their caller before anything is loaded, and they notify you of the results by invoking a callback function that you specify.

jQuery.getScript()

The `jQuery.getScript()` function takes the URL of a file of JavaScript code as its first argument. It asynchronously loads and then executes that code in the global scope. It can work for both same-origin and cross-origin scripts:

```
// Dynamically load a script from some other server
jQuery.getScript("http://example.com/js/widget.js");
```

You can pass a callback function as the second argument, and if you do, jQuery will invoke that function once after the code has been loaded and executed:

```
// Load a library and use it once it loads
jQuery.getScript("js/jquery.my_plugin.js", function() {
    $('div').my_plugin();  // Use the library we loaded
});
```

jQuery.getScript() normally uses an XMLHttpRequest object to fetch the text of the script to be executed. But for cross-domain requests (when the script is loaded by a server other than the one that served the current document), jQuery loads the script with a <script> tag. In the same-origin case, the first argument to your callback is the text of the script, the second argument is the status code "success", and the third argument is the XMLHttpRequest object used to fetch the text of the script. The return value of jQuery.getScript() is also the XMLHttpRequest object in this case. For cross-origin requests, there is no XMLHttpRequest object, and the text of the script is not captured. In this case, the callback function is called with its first and third arguments undefined, and the return value of jQuery.getScript() is also undefined.

The callback function you pass to jQuery.getScript() is invoked only if the request completes successfully. If you need to be notified of errors as well as successes, you'll need to use the lower-level jQuery.ajax() function. The same is true of the three other utility functions described in this section.

jQuery.getJSON()

jQuery.getJSON() is like jQuery.getScript(): it fetches text and then processes it specially before invoking the specified callback. Instead of executing the text as a script, jQuery.getJSON() parses it as JSON (using the jQuery.parseJSON() function; see Chapter 7 for more). jQuery.getJSON() is only useful when passed a callback argument. If the URL is loaded successfully and its content is parsed successfully as JSON, the resulting object will be passed as the first argument to the callback function. As with `jQuery.get Script()`, the second and third arguments to the callback are the status code "success" and the XMLHttpRequest object:

```
// Suppose data.json contains the text: '{"x":1,"y":2}'
jQuery.getJSON("data.json", function(data) {
    // Now data is the object {x:1, y:2}
});
```

Unlike `jQuery.getScript()`, `jQuery.getJSON()` accepts an optional data argument like the one passed to the `load()` method. If you pass data to `jQuery.getJSON()`, it must be the second argument and the callback must be the third. If you do not pass any data, the callback may be the second argument. If the data is a string, it is appended to the URL, following a ? or &. If the data is an object, it is converted to a string (see the following sidebar) and then appended to the URL.

If either the URL or data string passed to `jQuery.getJSON()` contains "=?" at the end of the string or before an ampersand, it is taken to specify a JSONP request. jQuery will replace the question mark with the name of a callback function it creates, and `jQuery.getJSON()` will then behave as if a script is being requested rather than a JSON object. This does not work for static JSON data files: it only works with server-side scripts that support JSONP. Because JSONP requests are handled as scripts, however, it does mean that JSON-formatted data can be requested cross-domain.

Passing Data to jQuery's Ajax Utilities

Most of jQuery's Ajax methods accept an argument (or an option) that specifies data to send to the server along with the URL. Usually this data takes the form of URL-encoded `name=value` pairs separated from each other by ampersands. (This data format is known by the MIME type "application/x-www-form-urlencoded". You can think of it as an analog of JSON: a format for converting simple JavaScript objects to and from strings.) For HTTP GET requests, this string of data is appended to the request URL. For POST requests, it is sent as the request body, after all the HTTP headers are sent.

One way to obtain a string of data in this format is to call the serialize() method of a jQuery object that contains forms or form elements. To submit an HTML form using the load() method, for example, you might use code like this:

```
$("#submit_button").click(function(e) {
    var f = this.form;       // The container form element
    $(f).load(               // Replace form by loading
        f.action,            // ...form url
        $(f).serialize());   // ...plus form data.
    e.preventDefault();      // Don't submit f normally
    this.disabled = "disabled"; // No more clicks
});
```

If you set the data argument (or option) of a jQuery Ajax function to an object rather than a string, jQuery will normally (with an exception described below) convert that object to a string by calling jQuery.param(). This utility function treats object properties as name=value pairs and converts the object {x:1,y:"hello"}, for example, to the string "x=1&y=hello".

In jQuery 1.4, jQuery.param() handles more complicated Java-Script objects. If the value of an object property is an array, each element of that array will have its own name/value pair in the resulting string, and the property name will have square brackets appended. And if the value of a property is an object, the property names of that nested object are placed in square brackets and appended to the outer property name:

```
$.param({a:[1,2,3]})        // "a[]=1&a[]=2&a[]=3"
$.param({o:{x:1,y:true}})   // "o[x]=1&o[y]=true"
$.param({o:{x:{y:[1]}}})    // "o[x][y][]=1
```

For backward compatibility with jQuery 1.3 and before, you can pass true as the second argument to jQuery.param() or set the traditional option to true. This will prevent the advanced serialization of properties whose values are arrays or objects.

Occasionally, you may want to pass a Document (or some other object that should not be automatically converted) as the body of a POST request. In this case, you can set the content Type option to specify the type of your data, and set the processData option to false to prevent jQuery from passing your data object to jQuery.param().

jQuery.get() and jQuery.post()

jQuery.get() and jQuery.post() fetch the content of the specified URL, passing the specified data, if any, and passing the result to the specified callback. jQuery.get() does this using an HTTP GET request, and jQuery.post() uses a POST request, but otherwise these two utility functions are the same. They both take the same three arguments as jQuery.getJSON(): a required URL, an optional data string or object, and a technically optional but almost always used callback function. The callback function is invoked with the returned data as its first argument, the string "success" as its second, and the XMLHttpRequest (if there was one) as its third.

```
// Request text and display it in an alert dialog
jQuery.get("debug.txt", alert);
```

In addition to the three arguments described above, these two methods accept a fourth optional argument (passed as the third argument if the data is omitted) that specifies the type of the data being requested. This fourth argument affects the way the data is processed before being passed to your callback. The load() method uses the type "html", jQuery.getScript() uses the type "script", and jQuery.getJSON() uses the type "json". jQuery.get() and jQuery.post() are more flexible than those special-purpose utilities, however, and you can specify any of these types. The legal values for this argument, as well as jQuery's behavior when you omit the argument, are explained in the following sidebar.

jQuery's Ajax Data Types

You can pass any of the following six types as an argument to jQuery.get() or jQuery.post(). And, as we'll see below, you can pass one of these types to jQuery.ajax() using the dataType option.

"text"

> This returns the server's response as plain text with no processing.

"html"

> This type works just like "text"—the response is plain text. The load() method uses this type and inserts the returned text into the document itself.

"xml"

> The URL is assumed to refer to XML-formatted data, and jQuery uses the responseXML property of the XMLHttpRequest object instead of the responseText property. The value passed to the callback is a Document object representing the XML document instead of a string holding the document text.

"script"

> The URL is assumed to reference a file of JavaScript, and the returned text is executed as a script before being passed to the callback. jQuery.getScript() uses this type. When the type is "script", jQuery can handle cross-domain requests using a <script> tag instead of an XMLHttpRequest object.

"json"

> The URL is assumed to reference a file of JSON-formatted data. The value passed to the callback is the object obtained by parsing the URL contents with jQuery.parseJSON() (see Chapter 7). jQuery.getJSON() uses this type. If the type is "json" and the URL or data string contains "=?", the type is converted to "jsonp".

"jsonp"

> The URL is assumed to refer to a server-side script that supports the JSONP protocol for passing JSON-formatted data as an argument to a client-specified function. This type passes the parsed object to the callback

function. Because JSONP requests can be made with
`<script>` tags, this type can be used to make cross-domain
requests, like the "script" type can. When you use this
type, your URL or data string should typically include a
parameter like "&jsonp=?" or "&callback=?". jQuery will
replace the question mark with the name of an automatically generated callback function. (But see the `jsonp` and
`jsonpCallback` options in "Uncommon Options and
Hooks" on page 78 for alternatives.)

If you do not specify one of these types when you invoke
jQuery.get(), jQuery.post(), or jQuery.ajax(), jQuery exam-
ines the Content-Type header of the HTTP response. If that
header includes the string "xml", an XML document is passed
to the callback. If the header includes the string "json", the
data is parsed as JSON and the parsed object is passed to the
callback. If it includes the string "javascript", the data is executed as a script. Otherwise, the data is treated as plain text.

The jQuery.ajax() Function

All of jQuery's Ajax utilities end up invoking jQuery.ajax()—
the most complicated function in the entire library.
jQuery.ajax() accepts just a single argument: an options object
whose properties specify many details about how to perform
the Ajax request. A call to jQuery.getScript(url,callback),
for example, is equivalent to this jQuery.ajax() invocation:

```
jQuery.ajax({
    type: "GET",        // The HTTP request method.
    url: url,           // The URL of the data to fetch.
    data: null,         // Don't add any data to the URL.
    dataType:"script",  // Execute response as a script.
    success: callback   // Call this function when done.
});
```

You can set these five fundamental options with
jQuery.get() and jQuery.post(). jQuery.ajax() supports quite
a few other options, however, if you invoke it directly. The

options (including the basic five shown above) are explained in detail below.

Before we dive into the options, note that you can set defaults for any of these options by passing an options object to `jQuery.ajaxSetup()`:

```
jQuery.ajaxSetup({
    // Abort all Ajax requests after 2 seconds
    timeout: 2000,
    // Defeat browser cache by adding a timestamp to URL
    cache: false
});
```

After running the code above, the specified **timeout** and **cache** options will be used for all Ajax requests (including high-level ones like `jQuery.get()` and the `load()` method) that do not specify their own values for these options.

While reading about jQuery's many options and callbacks in the sections that follow, you may find it helpful to refer to the sidebars about jQuery's Ajax status code and data type strings in "jQuery's Ajax Status Codes" on page 65 and "jQuery's Ajax Data Types" on page 71.

Common Options

The most commonly used `jQuery.ajax()` options are:

type

> This option specifies the HTTP request method. The default is "GET", but "POST" is another commonly used value. You can specify other HTTP request methods such as "DELETE" and "PUT" but not all browsers support them. Note that this option is misleadingly named: it has nothing to do with the data type of the request or response, and "method" would be a better name.

url

> The URL to be fetched. For GET requests, the **data** option will be appended to this URL. jQuery may add parameters to the URL for JSONP requests and for when the **cache** option is **false**.

data

> Data to be appended to the URL (for GET requests) or sent in the body of the request (for POST requests). This can be a string or an object. Objects are usually converted to strings as described in "Passing Data to jQuery's Ajax Utilities" on page 68, but see the processData option for an exception.

dataType

> Specifies the type of data expected in the response and how that data should be processed by jQuery. Legal values are "text", "html", "script", "json", "jsonp", and "xml". (The meanings of these values were explained in "jQuery's Ajax Data Types" on page 71.) This option has no default value. When left unspecified, jQuery examines the Content-Type header of the response to determine what to do with the returned data.

contentType

> This specifies the HTTP Content-Type header for the request. The default is "application/x-www-form-urlencoded", which is the normal value used by HTML forms and most server-side scripts. If you have set type to "POST" and want to send plain text or an XML document as the request body, you also need to set this option.

timeout

> A timeout, in milliseconds. If this option is set and the request has not completed within the specified timeout, the request will be aborted and the error callback will be called with status "timeout". The default timeout is 0, which means that requests continue until they complete and are never aborted.

cache

> For GET requests, if this option is set to false, jQuery will add a _= parameter to the URL or replace an existing parameter with that name. The value of this parameter is set to the current time (in millisecond format). This defeats browser-based caching since the URL will be different each time the request is made.

ifModified

When this option is set to **true**, jQuery records the values of the **Last-Modified** and **If-None-Match** response headers for each URL it requests, and then sets those headers in any subsequent requests for the same URL. This instructs the server to send an HTTP 304 "Not Modified" response if the URL has not changed since the last time it was requested. By default, this option is unset and jQuery does not set or record these headers.

jQuery translates an HTTP 304 response to the status code "notmodified". The "notmodified" status is not considered an error, and this value is passed to the **success** callback instead of the normal "success" status code. Thus if you set the **ifModified** option, you must check the status code in your callback—if the status is "notmodified", the first argument (the response data) will be undefined. Note that in versions of jQuery before 1.4, an HTTP 304 code was considered an error and the "notmodified" status code was passed to the **error** callback instead of the **success** callback. See "jQuery's Ajax Status Codes" on page 65 for more on jQuery's Ajax status codes.

global

This option specifies whether jQuery should trigger events that describe the progress of the Ajax request. The default is **true**; set this option to **false** to disable all Ajax-related events. (See "Ajax Events" on page 80 for full event details.) The name of this option is confusing: it is named "global" because jQuery normally triggers its events globally rather than on a specific object.

Callbacks

The following options specify functions to be invoked at various stages during the Ajax request. The **success** option is already familiar: it is the callback function that you pass to methods like **jQuery.getJSON()**. Note that jQuery also sends notification about the progress of an Ajax request as events (unless you have set the `global` option to `false`).

context

> This option specifies the object to be used as the context —the `this` value—for invocations of the various callback functions. This option has no default value, and if left unset, callbacks are invoked on the options object that holds them. Setting the `context` option also affects the way Ajax events are triggered (see "Ajax Events" on page 80). If you set it, the value should be a Window, Document, or Element on which events can be triggered.

beforeSend

> This option specifies a callback function that will be invoked before the Ajax request is sent to the server. The first argument is the XMLHttpRequest object, and the second is the options object for the request. The `before Send` callback gives programs the opportunity to set custom HTTP headers on the XMLHttpRequest object. If this callback function returns `false`, the Ajax request will be aborted. Note that cross-domain "script" and "jsonp" requests do not use an XMLHttpRequest object and do not trigger the `beforeSend` callback.

success

> This option specifies the callback function to be invoked when an Ajax request completes successfully. The first argument is the data sent by the server, the second argument is the jQuery status code, and the third is the XMLHttpRequest object that was used to make the request. As explained in "jQuery.get() and jQuery.post()" on page 70, the type of the first argument depends on the `dataType` option or on the `Content-Type` header of the server's response. If the type is "xml", the first argument is a Document object. If the type is "json" or "jsonp", the first argument is the object that results from parsing the server's JSON-formatted response. If the type was "script", the response is the text of the loaded script (that script will already have been executed,

however, so the response can usually be ignored in this case). For other types, the response is simply the text of the requested resource.

The second argument status code is normally the string "success", but if you have set the `ifModified` option, this argument might be "notmodified" instead. In this case, the server does not send a response and the first argument is undefined. Cross-domain requests of type "script" and "jsonp" are performed with a `<script>` tag instead of an XMLHttpRequest, so for those requests, the third argument will be undefined.

`error`

This option specifies the callback function to be invoked if the Ajax request does not succeed. The first argument to this callback is the XMLHttpRequest object of the request (if it used one). The second argument is the jQuery status code. This may be "error" for an HTTP error, "timeout" for a timeout, and "parsererror" for an error that occurred while parsing the server's response. If an XML document or JSON object is not well-formed, for example, the status code will be "parsererror". In this case, the third argument to the `error` callback will be the Error object that was thrown. Note that requests with `dataType` "script" that return invalid JavaScript code do not cause errors. Any errors in the script are silently ignored, and the `success` callback is invoked instead of the `error` callback.

`complete`

This option specifies a callback function to be invoked when the Ajax request is complete. Every Ajax request either succeeds and calls the `success` callback or fails and calls the `error` callback. jQuery invokes the `complete` callback after invoking either `success` or `error`. The first argument to the `complete` callback is the XMLHttpRequest object, and the second is the status code.

Uncommon Options and Hooks

The following Ajax options are uncommonly used. Some specify options that you are not likely to set, and others provide customization hooks if you need to modify jQuery's default handling of Ajax requests.

async

> Scripted HTTP requests are asynchronous by their very nature. The XMLHttpRequest object provides an option to block until the response is received, however. Set this option to **false** if you want jQuery to block. Setting this option does not change the return value of **jQuery.ajax()**: the function always returns the XMLHttpRequest object, if it used one. For synchronous requests, you can extract the server's response and HTTP status code from the XMLHttpRequest object yourself, or you can specify a **complete** callback (as you would for an asynchronous request) if you want jQuery's parsed response and status code.

dataFilter

> This option specifies a function to filter or preprocess the data returned by the server. The first argument will be the raw data from the server (either as a string or Document object for XML requests), and the second argument will be the value of the **dataType** option. If this function is specified, it must return a value, and that value will be used in place of the server's response. Note that the **data Filter** function is invoked before JSON parsing or script execution is performed. Also note that **dataFilter** is not invoked for cross-origin "script" and "jsonp" requests.

jsonp

> When you set the **dataType** option to "jsonp", your **url** or **data** option usually includes a parameter like "jsonp=?". If jQuery does not find such a parameter in the url or data, it inserts one, using this option as the parameter name. The default value of this option is "callback". Set this option if you are using JSONP with a server that expects a

different parameter name, and you have not yet encoded that parameter into your URL or data.

jsonpCallback

For requests with **dataType** "jsonp" (or type "json" when the URL includes a JSONP parameter like "jsonp=?"), jQuery must alter the URL to replace the question mark with the name of the wrapper function that the server will pass its data to. Normally, jQuery synthesizes a unique function name based on the current time. Set this option if you want to substitute your own function for jQuery's. If you do this, however, it will prevent jQuery from invoking the **success** and **complete** callbacks and from triggering its normal events.

processData

When you set the **data** option to an object (or pass an object as the second argument to **jQuery.get()** and related methods), jQuery normally converts that object to a string in the standard HTML "application/x-www-form-urlencoded" format (see "Passing Data to jQuery's Ajax Utilities" on page 68). If you want to avoid this step (such as when you want to pass a Document object as the body of a POST request), set this option to **false**.

scriptCharset

For cross-origin "script" and "jsonp" requests that use a **<script>** tag, this option specifies the value of the **charset** attribute of that tag. It has no effect for regular XMLHttpRequest-based requests.

traditional

jQuery 1.4 altered slightly the way that data objects were serialized to "application/x-www-form-urlencoded" strings (see "Passing Data to jQuery's Ajax Utilities" on page 68 for details). Set this option to **true** if you need jQuery to revert to its old behavior.

username, password

If a request requires password-based authentication, use these two options to specify the username and password.

xhr

> This option specifies a factory function for obtaining an XMLHttpRequest. It is invoked with no arguments and must return an object that implements the XMLHttpRequest API. This is a very low-level hook that allows you to create your own wrapper around XMLHttpRequest, adding features or instrumentation to its methods.

Ajax Events

"Callbacks" on page 75 explained that `jQuery.ajax()` has four callback options: `beforeSend`, `success`, `error`, and `complete`. In addition to invoking these individually specified callback functions, jQuery's `ajax` functions also fire custom events at each of the same stages in an Ajax request. The following table shows the callback options and the corresponding events:

Callback	Event Type	Handler Registration Method
beforeSend	"ajaxSend"	ajaxSend()
success	"ajaxSuccess"	ajaxSuccess()
error	"ajaxError"	ajaxError()
complete	"ajaxComplete"	ajaxComplete()
	"ajaxStart"	ajaxStart()
	"ajaxStop"	ajaxStop()

You can register handlers for these custom Ajax events using the `bind()` method (see "Advanced Event Handler Registration" on page 37) and the event type string shown in the second column, or using the event registration methods shown in the third column. `ajaxSuccess()` and the other methods work just like the `click()`, `mouseover()`, and other simple event registration methods of "Simple Event Handler Registration" on page 31.

Since these are custom events generated by jQuery rather than the browser, the Event object passed to the event handler does not contain much useful detail. The "ajaxSend", "ajaxSuccess", "ajaxError", and "ajaxComplete" events are all triggered with additional arguments, however. Handlers for these events will all be invoked with two extra arguments after the event. The first extra argument is the XMLHttpRequest object, and the second is the options object. This means, for example, that a handler for the "ajaxSend" event can add custom headers to an XMLHttpRequest object just like the **beforeSend** callback can. The "ajaxError" event is triggered with a third extra argument, in addition to the two just described. This final argument to the event handler is the Error object, if any, that was thrown when the error occurred. Surprisingly, these Ajax events are not passed jQuery's status code. If the handler for an "ajaxSuccess" event needs to distinguish "success" from "notmodified", for example, it will need to examine the raw HTTP status code in the XMLHttpRequest object.

The last two events listed in the table above are different from the others, most obviously because they have no corresponding callback functions, but also because they are triggered with no extra arguments. "ajaxStart" and "ajaxStop" indicate the start and stop of Ajax-related network activity. When jQuery is not performing any Ajax requests and a new request is initiated, it fires an "ajaxStart" event. If other requests begin before this first one ends, those new requests do not cause a new "ajaxStart" event. The "ajaxStop" event is triggered when the last pending Ajax request is completed and jQuery is no longer performing any network activity. This pair of events can be useful to show and hide some kind of "Loading..." animation or network activity icon. For example:

```
$("#loading_animation").bind({
    ajaxStart: function() { $(this).show(); },
    ajaxStop: function() { $(this).hide(); }
});
```

These "ajaxStart" and "ajaxStop" event handlers can be bound to any document element: jQuery triggers them globally (see "Triggering Events" on page 41) rather than on any one particular element. The other four Ajax events—"ajaxSend", "ajaxSuccess", "ajaxError", and "ajaxComplete"—are also normally triggered globally, so you can bind handlers to any element. If you set the `context` option in your call to `jQuery.ajax()`, however, these four events are triggered on the context element rather than globally.

Finally, remember that you can prevent jQuery from triggering any Ajax-related events by setting the `global` option to `false`. Despite its confusing name, setting `global` to `false` stops jQuery from triggering events on a `context` object, as well as stopping jQuery from triggering events globally.

CHAPTER 7

Utility Functions

The jQuery library defines a number of utility functions (as well as two properties) that you may find useful in your programs. As you'll see in the list below, a number of these functions now have equivalents in ECMAScript 5 (ES5). jQuery's functions predate ES5 and work in all browsers. In alphabetical order, the utility functions are:

jQuery.browser

The **browser** property is not a function, but an object that you can use for client sniffing or browser testing. This object will have the property **msie** set to **true** if the browser is IE. The **mozilla** property will be true if the browser is Firefox or related. The **webkit** property will be true for Safari and Chrome, and the **opera** property will be true for Opera. In addition to this browser-specific property, the **version** property contains the browser version number. Client sniffing is best avoided whenever possible, but you can use this property to work around browser-specific bugs with code like this:

```
if ($.browser.mozilla &&
    parseInt($.browser.version) < 4) {
    // Work around a hypothetical Firefox bug here.
}
```

`jQuery.contains()`

> This function expects two document elements as its arguments. It returns `true` if the first element contains the second element, and returns `false` otherwise.

`jQuery.each()`

> Unlike the `each()` method, which iterates only over jQuery objects, the `jQuery.each()` utility function iterates through the elements of an array or the properties of an object. The first argument is the array or object to be iterated. The second argument is the function to be called for each array element or object property. That function will be invoked with two arguments: the index or name of the array element or object property, and the value of the array element or object property. The `this` value for the function is the same as the second argument. If the function returns `false`, `jQuery.each()` returns immediately without completing the iteration. `jQuery.each()` always returns its first argument.

> `jQuery.each()` enumerates object properties with an ordinary `for/in` loop, so all enumerable properties are iterated, even inherited properties. `jQuery.each()` enumerates array elements in numerical order by index and does not skip the undefined properties of sparse arrays.

`jQuery.extend()`

> This function expects objects as its arguments. It copies the properties of the second and subsequent objects into the first object, overwriting any properties with the same name in the first argument. This function skips any properties whose value is `undefined` or `null`. If only one object is passed, the properties of that object are copied into the `jQuery` object itself. The return value is the object into which properties were copied. If the first argument is the value `true`, a deep or recursive copy is performed: the second argument is extended with the properties of the third (and any subsequent) objects.

This function is useful for cloning objects and for merging options objects with sets of defaults:

```
var clone = jQuery.extend({}, original);
var opts = jQuery.extend({}, defaults, user_opts);
```

jQuery.globalEval()

This function executes a string of JavaScript code in the global context, as if it were the contents of a `<script>` tag. (In fact, jQuery actually implements this function by creating a `<script>` tag and temporarily inserting it into the document.)

jQuery.grep()

This function is like the ES5 `filter()` method of the Array object. It expects an array as its first argument and a predicate function as its second, and it invokes the predicate once for each element in the array, passing the element value and the element index. jQuery.grep() returns a new array that contains only those elements of the argument array for which the predicate returned **true** (or another truthy value). If you pass **true** as the third argument to jQuery.grep(), it inverts the sense of the predicate and returns an array of elements for which the predicate returned **false** (or another falsy value).

jQuery.inArray()

This function is like the ES5 `indexOf()` method of the Array object. It expects an arbitrary value as its first argument and an array (or array-like object) as its second, and it returns the first index in the array at which the value appears, or -1 if the array does not contain the value.

jQuery.isArray()

Returns **true** if the argument is a native Array object.

jQuery.isEmptyObject

Returns **true** if the argument has no enumerable properties.

jQuery.isFunction()

Returns **true** if the argument is a native Function object. Note that in IE 8 and earlier, browser methods like

`Window.alert()` and `Element.attachEvent()` are not functions in this sense.

`jQuery.isPlainObject()`

Returns **true** if the argument is a "plain" object rather than an instance of some more specialized type or class of objects.

`jQuery.makeArray()`

If the argument is an array-like object, this function copies the elements of that object into a new (true) array and returns that array. If the argument is not array-like, this function simply returns a new array with the argument as its single element.

`jQuery.map()`

This function is like the ES5 `map()` method of the Array object. It expects an array or array-like object as its first argument and a function as its second. It passes each array element along with the index of that element to the function, and it returns a new array that collects the values returned by the function. `jQuery.map()` differs from the ES5 `map()` method in a couple of ways. If your mapping function returns **null**, that value will not be included in the result array. And if your mapping function returns an array, the elements of that array will be added to the result rather than the array itself.

`jQuery.merge()`

This function expects two arrays or array-like objects. It appends the elements of the second to the first and returns the first. The first array is modified, the second is not. Note that you can use this function to shallowly clone an array like this:

```
var clone = jQuery.merge([], original);
```

`jQuery.parseJSON()`

This function parses a JSON-formatted string and returns the resulting value. It throws an exception when passed malformed input. jQuery uses the standard `JSON.parse()` function in browsers that define it. Note that jQuery defines only a JSON parsing function, not a JSON serialization function.

jQuery.proxy()

This function is something like the ES5 `bind()` method of the Function object. It takes a function as its first argument and an object as its second, and it returns a new function that invokes the function as a method of the object. It does not perform partial application of arguments like the `bind()` method does.

`jQuery.proxy()` can also be invoked with an object as its first argument and a property name as its second. The value of the named property should be a function. Invoked this way, `jQuery.proxy(o,n)` returns the same thing as `jQuery.proxy(o[n],o)`.

`jQuery.proxy()` is intended for use with jQuery's event handler binding mechanism. If you bind a proxied function, you can unbind it using the original function.

jQuery.support

This is a property like `jQuery.browser`, but it is intended for portable feature testing rather than more brittle browser testing. The value of `jQuery.support` is an object whose properties are all boolean values that specify the presence or absence of browser features. Most of these `jQuery.support` properties are low-level details used internally by jQuery. They may be of interest to plugin writers, but most are not generally useful to application writers. One exception is `jQuery.support.boxModel`: this property is `true` if the browser uses the CSS standard "context-box" model, and is `false` in IE 6 and IE 7 in quirks mode.

jQuery.trim()

This function is like the `trim()` method added to strings in ES5. It expects a string as its only argument and returns a copy of that string with leading and trailing whitespace removed.

CHAPTER 8

Selectors and Selection Methods

We've been using the jQuery selection function, $(), with simple CSS selectors. It is now time to study the jQuery selector grammar in depth, along with a number of methods for refining and augmenting the set of selected elements.

jQuery Selectors

jQuery supports a fairly complete subset of the selector grammar defined by the CSS3 Selectors draft standard, with the addition of some nonstandard but very useful pseudoclasses.

The selector grammar has three layers. You've undoubtedly seen the simplest kind of selectors before. "#test" selects an element with an `id` attribute of "test", "blockquote" selects all `<blockquote>` tags in the document, and "div.note" selects all `<div>` tags with a `class` attribute of "note". Simple selectors can be combined into "selector combinations" such as "div.note>p" and "blockquote i" by separating them with a *combinator* character. And simple selectors and selector combinations can be grouped into comma-separated lists. These selector groups are the most general kind of selector that we pass to $(). Before explaining selector combinations and selector groups, we must explain the syntax of simple selectors.

Simple Selectors

A simple selector begins (explicitly or implicitly) with a tag type specification. If you are only interested in `<p>` tags, for example, your simple selector would begin with "p". If you want to select elements without regard to their tagname, use the wildcard "*" instead. If a selector does not begin with either a tagname or a wildcard, the wildcard is implicit.

The tagname or wildcard specifies an initial set of document elements that are candidates for selection. The portion of the simple selector that follows this type specification consists of zero or more filters. The filters are applied left-to-right, in the order that they appear, and each one narrows the set of selected elements. Table 8-1 lists the filters supported by jQuery.

Table 8-1. jQuery Selector Filters

Filter	Meaning
#id	Matches the element with an id attribute of id. Valid HTML documents never have more than one element with the same id, so this filter is usually used as a standalone selector.
.class	Matches any elements whose class attribute (when interpreted as a list of words separated by spaces) includes the word class.
[attr]	Matches any elements that have an attr attribute (regardless of its value).
[attr=val]	Matches any elements that have an attr attribute whose value is val.
[attr!=val]	Matches elements that have no attr attribute, or whose attr attribute is not equal to val (jQuery extension).
[attr^=val]	Matches elements whose attr attribute has a value that begins with val.
[attr$=val]	Matches elements whose attr attribute has a value that ends with val.

Filter	Meaning
[*attr**=*val*]	Matches elements whose *attr* attribute has a value that contains *val*.
[*attr*~=*val*]	Matches elements whose *attr* attribute, when interpreted as a list of words separated by spaces, includes the word *val*. Thus the selector "div.note" is the same as "div[class~=note]".
[*attr*|=*val*]	Matches elements whose *attr* attribute has a value that begins with *val* and is optionally followed by a hyphen and any other character.
:animated	Matches elements that are currently being animated by jQuery.
:button	Matches <button type="button"> and <input type="button"> elements (jQuery extension).
:checkbox	Matches <input type="checkbox"> elements (jQuery extension). This filter is most efficient when explicitly prefixed with the input tag: "input:checkbox".
:checked	Matches input elements that are checked.
:contains(*text*)	Matches elements that contain the specified *text* (jQuery extension). The parentheses of this filter delimit the text— no quotation marks are required. The text of the elements being filtered is determined with their textContent or innerText properties—this is the raw document text, with tags and comments stripped out.
:disabled	Matches disabled elements.
:empty	Matches elements that have no children, including no text content.
:enabled	Matches elements that are not disabled.
:eq(*n*)	Matches only the *n*th element of the document-order zero-indexed list of matches (jQuery extension).
:even	Matches elements with even indexes in the list. Since the first element has an index of 0, this actually matches the first, third, and fifth (and so on) elements (jQuery extension).
:file	Matches <input type="file"> elements (jQuery extension).

Filter	Meaning
:first	Matches only the first element in the list. Same as :eq(0) (jQuery extension).
:first-child	Matches only elements that are the first child of their parent. Note that this is completely different than :first.
:gt(n)	Matches elements in the document-order list of matches whose zero-based index is greater than n (jQuery extension).
:has(sel)	Matches elements that have a descendant matching the nested selector sel.
:header	Matches any header tag: <h1>, <h2>, <h3>, <h4>, <h5>, or <h6> (jQuery extension).
:hidden	Matches any element that is not visible on the screen: roughly those elements whose offsetWidth and offsetHeight are 0.
:image	Matches <input type="image"> elements. Note that this does not match <img> tags (jQuery extension).
:input	Matches user input elements: <input>, <textarea>, <select>, and <button> (jQuery extension).
:last	Matches the last element in the list of matches (jQuery extension).
:last-child	Matches any element that is the last child of its parent. Note that this is not the same as :last.
:lt(n)	Matches all elements in the document-order list of matches whose zero-based index is less than n (jQuery extension).
:not(sel)	Matches elements that are *not* matched by the nested selector sel.
:nth(n)	A synonym for :eq(n) (jQuery extension).
:nth-child(n)	Matches elements that are the nth child of their parent. n can be a number, the word "even", the word "odd", or a formula. Use :nth-child(even) to select elements that are the second and fourth (and so on) in their parents' list of children. Use :nth-child(odd) to select elements that are first, third, and so on.
	Most generally, n can be a formula of the form xn or xn+y, where x and y are integers and n is the literal letter n. Thus

Filter	Meaning
	nth-child(3n+1) selects the first, fourth, and seventh (and so on) elements.
	Note that this filter uses one-based indexes, so an element that is the first child of its parent is considered odd and is matched by 3n+1, not 3n. Contrast this with the :even and :odd filters that are based on an element's zero-based position in the list of matches.
:odd	Matches elements with odd (zero-based) indexes in the list. Note that elements 1 and 3 are the 2nd and 4th matched element, respectively (jQuery extension).
:only-child	Matches elements that are the only child of their parent.
:parent	Matches elements that are parents. This is the opposite of :empty (jQuery extension).
:password	Matches <input type="password"> elements (jQuery extension).
:radio	Matches <input type="radio"> elements (jQuery extension).
:reset	Matches <input type="reset"> and <button type="reset"> elements (jQuery extension).
:selected	Matches <option> tags that are selected. Use :checked for selected checkboxes and radio buttons (jQuery extension).
:submit	Matches <input type="submit"> and <button type="submit"> elements (jQuery extension).
:text	Matches <input type="text"> elements (jQuery extension).
:visible	Matches all elements that are currently visible: roughly those that have non-zero offsetWidth and offsetHeight. This is the opposite of :hidden.

Notice that some of the filters listed in Table 8-1 accept arguments within parentheses. The following selector, for example, selects paragraphs that are the first or every third subsequent child of their parent, as long as they contain the word "Java-Script" and do not contain an <a> tag:

```
p:nth-child(3n+1):text(JavaScript):not(:has(a))
```

Filters typically run most efficiently if prefixed with a tag type. Rather than simply using ":radio" to select radio buttons, for example, it is better to use "input:radio". The exception is id filters, which are most efficient when they stand alone. The selector "#address" is typically more efficient than the more explicit "form#address", for example.

Selector Combinations

Simple selectors can be combined to use special operators or combinators to represent relationships between elements in the document tree. Table 8-2 lists the selector combinations supported by jQuery. These are the same selector combinations that CSS3 supports.

Table 8-2. jQuery Selector Combinations

Combination	Meaning
A B	Selects document elements matching selector B that are descendants of elements that match selector A. Note that the combinator character is simply whitespace for this combination.
A > B	Selects document elements that match selector B that are direct children of elements that match selector A.
A + B	Selects document elements that match selector B and immediately follow (ignoring text nodes and comments) elements that match selector A.
A ~ B	Selects document elements matching B that are sibling elements that come after elements that match A.

Here are some example selector combinations:

```
"blockquote i"     // Matches <i> within a <blockquote>
"ol > li"          // <li> as a direct child of <ol>
"#output + *"      // The sibling after the #output elt
"div.note > h1 + p" // <p> after <h1> inside a div.note
```

Note that selector combinations are not limited to combinations of two selectors: three or more selectors are allowed, too. Selector combinations are processed left-to-right.

Selector Groups

A selector group, which is the kind of selector that we pass to $() (or use in a stylesheet), is simply a comma-separated list of one or more simple selectors or selector combinations. A selector group matches all elements that match any of the selector combinations in the group. For our purposes here, even a simple selector can be considered a selector combination. Here are some example selector groups:

```
"h1, h2, h3"      // All <h1>, <h2> and <h3> tags
"#p1, #p2, #p3"   // Elements with id p1, p2 and p3
"div.note, p.note" // Any <div> or <p> with class="note"
"body>p,div.note>p" // <p> children of <body> or div.note
```

Note that the CSS and jQuery selector syntax use parentheses for some of the filters in simple selectors, but they do not allow parentheses to be used more generally for grouping. You cannot put a selector group or selector combination in parentheses and treat it like a simple selector, for example:

```
(h1, h2, h3)+p    // Not legal
h1+p, h2+p, h3+p  // Write this instead
```

Selection Methods

In addition to the selector grammar supported by $(), jQuery defines a number of selection methods. Most of the jQuery methods we've seen so far in this chapter perform some action on the selected elements. The selection methods are different: they alter the set of selected elements by refining it, augmenting it, or just using it as a starting point for a new selection.

This section describes these selection methods. You'll notice that many of the methods provide the same functionality as the selector grammar itself.

The simplest way to refine a selection is by its position within the selection. first() returns the jQuery object that contains only the first selected element, and last() returns the jQuery object that contains only the last element. More generally, the eq() method returns a jQuery object that contains only the single selected element at the specified index. (In jQuery 1.4, negative indexes are allowed and count from the end of the selection.) Note that these methods return a jQuery object with a single element. This is different than regular array indexing, which returns a single element with no jQuery object wrapped around it:

```
var paras = $("p");
paras.first()        // Select only the first <p> tag
paras.last()         // Select only the last <p>
paras.eq(1)          // Select the second <p>
paras.eq(-2)         // Select the second to last <p>
paras[1]             // The second <p> tag, itself
```

The general method for refining a selection by position is slice(). The jQuery slice() method works like the Array.slice() method: it accepts a start and an end index (with negative indexes measured from the end of the array), and returns a jQuery object that contains elements from the start index up to, but not including, the end index. If the end index is omitted, the returned object includes all elements at or after the start index:

```
$("p").slice(2,5)    // The 3rd, 4th and 5th <p> tags
$("div").slice(-3)   // The last three <div> tags
```

filter() is a general-purpose selection filtering method, and you can invoke it in three different ways:

- If you pass a selector string to filter(), it returns a jQuery object containing only those selected elements that also match that selector.

- If you pass another jQuery object to filter(), it returns a new jQuery object that contains the intersection of the two jQuery objects. You can also pass an array of elements, or even a single document element, to filter().

- If you pass a predicate function to filter(), that function is called for each matched element, and filter() returns a jQuery object containing only those elements for which the predicate returned true (or any truthy value). The predicate function is called with the element as its this value, and the element index as an argument. (See also jQuery.grep() in Chapter 7.)

```
$("div").filter(".note")       // Like $("div.note")
$("div").filter($(".note"))    // Like $("div.note")
$("div").filter(function(i) {  // Like $("div:even")
    return i % 2 == 0
})
```

The not() method is just like filter() except that it inverts the sense of the filter. If you pass a selector string to not(), it returns a new jQuery object containing only the selected elements that do *not* match the selector. If you pass a jQuery object or an array of elements or a single element, not() returns all of the selected elements except for those elements you've explicitly excluded. If you pass a predicate function to not(), it is invoked just as it is for filter(), but the returned jQuery object includes only those elements for which the predicate returns false (or a falsy value):

```
// All <div> tags except two special ones
$("div").not("#header, #footer");
```

In jQuery 1.4, the has() method is another way to refine a selection. If you pass a selector, it returns a new jQuery object that contains only the selected elements that have a descendant that matches the selector. If you pass a document element to has(), it refines the selection to match only those elements that are ancestors of the specified element:

```
$("p").has("a[href]")  // Paragraphs that include links
```

The add() method augments a selection rather than filtering or refining it. You can invoke add() with any arguments (other than a function) that you would pass to $(). add() returns the originally selected elements, plus whatever elements would be selected (or created) by the arguments if those arguments were passed to $(). add() removes duplicate elements and sorts the combined selection so that elements are in document order:

```
// Equivalent ways to select all <div> and <p> elements
$("div, p")             // Use a selector group
$("div").add("p")       // Pass a selector to add()
$("div").add($("p"))    // Pass a jQuery object to add()
```

```
var paras = document.getElementsByTagName("p");
$("div").add(paras);    // Pass an array-like object
```

Using a Selection As Context

The filter(), add(), and not() methods described above perform set intersection, union, and subtraction operations on
independent selections. jQuery defines a number of other selection methods that use the current selection as the context.
For each selected element, these methods make a new selection
using the selected element as the context or starting point, and
then return a new jQuery object that contains the union of
those selections. As with the add() method, duplicates are removed and the elements are sorted so that they are in document
order.

The most general of this category of selection methods is
find(). It searches the descendants of each of the currently selected elements for elements that match the specified selector
string, and returns a new jQuery object that represents that
new set of matching descendants. Note that the newly selected
elements are not merged with the existing selection; they are
returned as a new set of elements. Note also that find() is not
the same as filter(), which simply narrows the currently selected set of elements without selecting new elements:

```
// find <p> tags inside <div> tags.  Same as $("div p")
$("div").find("p")
```

The other methods in this category return new jQuery objects
that represent the children, siblings, or parents of each of the
currently selected elements. Most accept an optional selector
string as an argument. With no selector, they return all appropriate children, siblings, or parents. With the selector, they filter the list to return only those that match.

The children() method returns the immediate child elements
of each selected element, filtering them with an optional
selector:

```
// Find all <span> tags that are direct children of the
// elements with ids "header" and "footer".
// Same as $("#header>span,#footer>span")
$("#header, #footer").children("span")
```

The contents() method is similar to children() but it returns
all child nodes, including text nodes, of each element. Also, if
any of the selected elements is an <iframe>, contents() returns
the document object for the content of that <iframe>. Note that
contents() does not accept an optional selector string—this is
because it returns document nodes that are not elements, and
selector strings only describe element nodes.

The next() and prev() methods return the next and previous
sibling of each selected element that has one. If a selector is
specified, the sibling is selected only if it matches the selector:

```
$("h1").next("p") // Same as $("h1+p")
$("h1").prev()    // Sibling elements before <h1> tags
```

nextAll() and prevAll() return all siblings following and preceding (if there are any) each selected element. And the
siblings() method returns all siblings of each selected element
(elements are not considered siblings of themselves). If a selector is passed to any of these methods, only siblings that
match are returned:

```
// All <p> siblings following the #footer element
$("#footer").nextAll("p")
// All siblings before the #footer element
$("#footer").prevAll()
```

In jQuery 1.4 and later, the nextUntil() and prevUntil() methods take a selector argument and select all siblings following
or preceding the selected element until a sibling is found that
matches the selector. If you omit the selector, these methods
work just like nextAll() and prevAll() with no selector.

The parent() method returns the parent of each selected
element:

```
$("li").parent() // Elements that have <li> children
```

The `parents()` method returns the ancestors (up to the `<html>` tag) of each selected element. Both `parent()` and `parents()` accept an optional selector string argument:

```
$("a[href]").parents("p") // <p> tags that contain links
```

`parentsUntil()` returns the ancestors of each selected element until the first ancestor that matches the specified selector. The `closest()` method requires a selector string, and it returns the closest ancestor (if any) of each selected element that matches the selector. For this method, an element is considered an ancestor of itself. In jQuery 1.4, you can also pass an ancestor element as the second argument to `closest()` to prevent jQuery from climbing the ancestor tree beyond the specified element:

```
// Innermost <div>s that contain links
$("a[href]").closest("div")
// All <div> wrappers directly around <a>
$("a[href]").parentsUntil(":not(div)")
```

Reverting to a Previous Selection

To facilitate method chaining, most jQuery object methods return the object on which they are called. However, the methods we've covered in this section all return new jQuery objects. Method chaining works but you must keep in mind that methods called later in the chain may be operating on a different set of elements than those near the start of the chain.

The situation is a little more complicated than this, however. When the selection methods described here create and return a new jQuery object, they give that object an internal reference to the older jQuery object from which it was derived. This creates a linked list or stack of jQuery objects. The `end()` method pops this stack, returning the saved jQuery object. Calling `end()` in a method chain restores the set of matched elements to its previous state. Consider the following code:

```
// Find all <div> tags, then find the <p> tags inside.
// Highlight the <p> tags and then give the <div> tags
// a border. First, without method chaining:
var divs = $("div");
var paras = divs.find("p");
```

```
paras.addClass("highlight");
divs.css("border", "solid black 1px");

// Here's how we could do it with a method chain
$("div").find("p").addClass("highlight")
    .end().css("border", "solid black 1px");

// Or reorder the operations and avoid the call to end()
$("div").css("border", "solid black 1px")
    .find("p").addClass("highlight");
```

If you ever want to manually modify the set of selected elements in a way that is compatible with the end() method, pass the new set of elements as an array or array-like object to the push Stack() method. The elements you specify become the new selected elements, and the previous set of selected elements are pushed on the stack, where they can be restored with end():

```
var sel = $("div");    // Select all <div> tags
var paras = document.getElementsByTagName("p");
sel.pushStack(paras); // Modify selection to all <p>s
sel.end();             // Restore selection to all <div>s
```

Now that we've covered the end() method and the selection stack that it uses, there is one final method to cover. and Self() returns a new jQuery object that includes all of the elements of the current selection plus all of the elements (minus duplicates) of the previous selection. andSelf() works like the add() method, so "addPrev" might be a more descriptive name for it. As an example, consider the following variant on the code above: it highlights <p> tags and the <div> tags that hold them, and then adds a border to the <div> tags:

```
$("div").find("p")             // find <p>s in <div>s
    .andSelf()                 // merge them together
    .addClass("highlight")     // Highlight them all
    .end().end()               // Pop twice back to $("div")
    .css("border", "solid black 1px"); // Add a border
```

CHAPTER 9

Extending jQuery with Plugins

jQuery is written so that it is easy to add new functionality. Modules that add new functionality are called *plugins*, and you can find many of them at *http://plugins.jquery.com*. jQuery plugins are just ordinary files of JavaScript code, and to use them in your web pages, you just include them with a `<script>` tag as you would any other JavaScript library (you must include plugins after you include jQuery itself, of course).

It is almost trivially easy to write your own jQuery extensions. The trick is to know that `jQuery.fn` is the prototype object for all jQuery objects. If you add a function to this object, that function becomes a jQuery method. Here is an example:

```
jQuery.fn.println = function() {
    // Join arguments into a space-separated string
    var msg = Array.prototype.join.call(arguments, " ");
    // Loop through each element in the jQuery object
    this.each(function() {
        // For each one, append the string as plain text,
        jQuery(this).append(document.createTextNode(msg))
            .append("<br/>");  // then append a <br/>.
    });
    // Return the jQuery object for method chaining
    return this;
};
```

With that `jQuery.fn.println` function defined, we can now invoke a `println()` method on any jQuery object:

```
$("#debug").println("x = ", x, "; y = ", y);
```

It is common practice to add new methods to `jQuery.fn`. If you use the `each()` method to "manually" iterate through the elements in a jQuery object and perform some kind of operation on them, consider whether it might make sense to refactor your code so that the `each()` invocation is moved into an extension method. If you follow basic modular coding practices when writing your extension, and abide by a few jQuery-specific conventions, you can call your extension a plugin and share it with others. These are the jQuery plugin conventions to be aware of:

- Don't rely on the `$` identifier: the including page may have called `jQuery.noConflict()`, and `$()` may no longer be a synonym for the `jQuery()` function. In short plugins like the one shown above, you can just use `jQuery` instead of `$`. If you are writing a longer extension, you are likely to wrap it all within one anonymous function to avoid the creation of global variables. If you do so, you can use the idiom of passing the jQuery as an argument to your anonymous function and receiving that value in a parameter named `$`:

  ```
  (function($) { // An function with parameter named $
      // Put your plugin code here
  }(jQuery)); // Pass the jQuery object to the function
  ```

- If your extension method does not return a value of its own, be sure to return a jQuery object that can be used in a method chain. Usually this will just be the `this` object, which you can return unmodified. In the example above, the method ended with the line `return this;`. The method could have been made slightly shorter (and less readable) following another jQuery idiom: returning the result of the `each()` method. Then the `println()` method would have included the code `return this.each(function() {...});`.

- If your extension method has more than a couple of parameters or configuration options, allow the user to pass options in the form of an object (as we saw with the `animate()` method in "Custom Animations" on page 53, and the `jQuery.ajax()` function in "The jQuery.ajax() Function" on page 72).

- Don't pollute the jQuery method namespace. Well-behaved jQuery plugins define the smallest number of methods consistent with a usable API. It is common for jQuery plugins to define only a single method in `jQuery.fn`. This one method takes a string as its first argument and interprets that string as the name of a function to pass its remaining arguments to. When you are able to limit your plugin to a single method, the name of that method should be the same as the name of the plugin. If you must define more than one method, use the plugin name as a prefix for each of your method names.

- If your plugin binds event handlers, put all of those handlers in an event namespace (see "Advanced Event Handler Registration" on page 37). Use your plugin name as the namespace name.

- If your plugin uses the `data()` method to associate data with elements, place all of your data values in a single object, and store that object as a single value, giving it the same name as your plugin.

- Save your plugin code in a file with a name of the form "jquery.*plugin*.js", replacing *plugin* with the name of your plugin.

A plugin can add new utility functions to jQuery by adding them to the jQuery object itself. For example:

```
// This method prints its arguments (using the println()
// plugin method) to the element with id "debug". If no
// such element exists, it is created and added.
jQuery.debug = function() {
    // Find the #debug element
    var elt = jQuery("#debug");
    // Create and insert it if necessary
    if (elt.length === 0) {
```

```
        elt = jQuery("<div id='debug'>" +
                    "<h1>Debugging Output</h1></div>");
        jQuery(document.body).append(elt);
    }
    // Output the arguments to it
    elt.println.apply(elt, arguments);
};
```

In addition to defining new methods, it is also possible to extend other parts of the jQuery library. In Chapter 5, for example, we saw that it is possible to add new effect duration names (in addition to "fast" and "slow") by adding properties to jQuery.fx.speeds, and that it is possible to add new easing functions by adding them to jQuery.easing. Plugins can even extend the jQuery CSS selector engine! You can add new pseudoclass filters (like :first and :input) by adding properties to the jQuery.expr[':'] object. Here is an example that defines a new :draggable filter, which returns only elements that have a draggable=true attribute:

```
jQuery.expr[':'].draggable = function(e) {
    return e.draggable === true;
};
```

With this selector defined, we can select draggable images with $("img:draggable") instead of the more verbose $("img[draggable=true]").

As you can see from the code above, a custom selector function is passed a candidate DOM element as its first argument. It should return true if the element matches the selector, and false otherwise. Many custom selectors need only the one element argument, but they are actually invoked with four arguments. The second argument is an integer index that gives the element's position within an array of candidate elements. That array is passed as the fourth argument, and your selector must not modify it. The third argument is interesting: it is the array result of a call to the RegExp.exec() method. The fourth element of this array (at index 3) is the value, if any, within parentheses after the pseudoclass filter. The parentheses and any quotes inside are stripped, leaving only the argument string. Here, for example, is how you could implement a :data(x) pseudoclass that returns **true** only for arguments that have an HTML5 data-x attribute:

```
jQuery.expr[':'].data = function(e, idx, match, array) {
    return e.hasAttribute("data-" + match[3]);
};
```

CHAPTER 10

The jQuery UI Library

jQuery limits itself to providing core DOM, CSS, event handling, and Ajax functionality. These provide an excellent foundation for building higher-level abstractions, such as user interface widgets, and the jQuery UI library does just that. Full coverage of jQuery UI is beyond the scope of this book, but this chapter offers a simple overview. You can find the library and its documentation at *http://jqueryui.com*.

As its name implies, jQuery UI defines a number of user interface widgets: auto-completion input fields, date pickers for entering dates, accordions and tabs for organizing information, sliders and progress bars for visually displaying numbers, and modal dialogs for urgent communication with the user. In addition to these widgets, jQuery UI implements more general "interactions", which allow any document element to be easily made draggable, droppable, resizable, selectable, or sortable. Finally, jQuery UI adds a number of new visual effects methods (including the ability to animate colors) to those offered by jQuery itself, and defines lots of new easing functions as well.

Think of jQuery UI as a bunch of related jQuery plugins packed into a single JavaScript file. To use it, simply include the jQuery UI script into your web page after including the jQuery code. The Download page at *http://jqueryui.com* allows you to select the components you plan to use, and will build a custom download bundle for you that may reduce your page load times compared to the full jQuery UI library.

jQuery UI is fully themeable, and its themes take the form of CSS files. So in addition to loading the jQuery UI JavaScript code into your web pages, you'll have to include the CSS file for your selected theme as well. The jQuery UI website features a number of prebuilt themes and also a "ThemeRoller" page that allows you to customize and download your own theme.

jQuery UI widgets and interactions are structured as jQuery plugins, and each defines a single jQuery method. Typically, when you call this method on an existing document element, it transforms that element into the widget. For example, to alter a text input field so that it pops up a date picker widget when clicked or focused, simply call the **datepicker()** method with code like this:

```
// Make input.date tags into date picker widgets
$("input.date").datepicker();
```

In order to make full use of a jQuery UI widget, you must be familiar with three things: its configuration options, its methods, and its events. All jQuery UI widgets are configurable, and some have many configuration options. You can customize the behavior and appearance of your widgets by passing an options object (like the animations options object passed to **animate()**) to the widget method.

jQuery UI widgets usually define at least a handful of "methods" for interacting with the widget. In order to avoid a proliferation of jQuery methods, however, jQuery UI widgets do not define their "methods" as true methods. Each widget has only a single method (like the **datepicker()** method in the example above). When you want to call a "method" of the widget, you pass the name of the desired "method" to the single true method defined by the widget. To disable a date picker widget, for example, you don't call **disableDatepicker()**; instead, you call **datepicker("disable")**.

jQuery UI widgets generally define custom events that they trigger in response to user interaction. You can bind event handlers for these custom events with the normal `bind()` method, and you can also usually specify event handler functions as properties in the options object you pass to the widget method. The first argument to these handler methods is an Event object as usual. Some widgets pass a "UI" object as the second argument to the event handler, which typically provides state information about the widget.

Note that the jQuery UI documentation sometimes describes "events" that are not truly custom events and could better be described as callback functions set through the configuration options object. The date picker widget, for example, supports a number of callback functions that it can call at various times. None of these functions have the standard event handler signature, however, and you cannot register handlers for these "events" with `bind()`. Instead, you specify appropriate callbacks when you configure the widget in your initial call to the `datepicker()` method.

jQuery Quick Reference

This is a quick reference for the entire jQuery library. jQuery functions and methods are listed by category and are briefly described in the sections that follow.

This reference uses the following conventions in the method signatures. Arguments named *sel* are jQuery selectors. Arguments named *idx* are integer indexes. Arguments named *elt* or *elts* are document elements or array-like objects of document elements. Arguments named *f* are callback functions, and nested parentheses are used to indicate the arguments that jQuery will pass to the function you supply. Square brackets indicate optional arguments. If an optional argument is followed by an equals sign and a value, that value will be used when the argument is omitted. The return value of a function or a method follows the close parenthesis and a colon. Methods with no return value specified return the jQuery object on which they are invoked.

Factory Function

The `jQuery()` function is a namespace for a variety of utility functions, but it is also the factory function for creating jQuery objects. `jQuery()` can be invoked in all of the ways shown below, but it always returns a jQuery object that represents a collection of document elements (or the Document object itself). The symbol **$** is an alias for **jQuery**, and you can use **$()** instead of **jQuery()** in each of the forms below:

jQuery(*sel* [, *context*=document])

> Returns a new jQuery object that represents the document elements that are descendants of *context* and match the selector string *sel*.

jQuery(*elts*)

> Returns a new jQuery object that represents the specified elements. *elts* may be a single document element or an array or array-like object (such as a NodeList or another jQuery object) of document elements.

jQuery(*html*, [*props*])

> Parses *html* as a string of HTML-formatted text, and returns a new jQuery object that contains one or more top-level elements in the string. If *html* describes a single HTML tag, *props* may be an object that specifies HTML attributes and event handlers for the newly created element.

jQuery(*f*)

> Registers *f* as a function to be invoked when the document has loaded and is ready to be manipulated. If the document is already ready, *f* is invoked immediately as a method of the document object. Returns a jQuery object that contains only the document object.

Selector Grammar

The jQuery selector grammar is very similar to that of CSS3, and it is explained in detail in "jQuery Selectors" on page 89. The following is a summary:

Simple tag, class, and id selectors

> `*`   `tagname`   `.classname`   `#id`

Selector combinations

> `A B`   *B as a descendant of A*
> `A > B`   *B as a child of A*

```
A + B    B as a sibling following A
A ~ B    B as a sibling of A
```

Attribute filters

```
[attr]        has attribute
[attr=val]    has attribute with value val
[attr!=val]   does not have attribute with value val
[attr^=val]   attribute begins with val
[attr$=val]   attribute ends with val
[attr*=val]   attribute includes val
[attr~=val]   attribute includes val as a word
[attr|=val]   attribute begins with val and optional hyphen
```

Element type filters

```
:button     :header    :password   :submit
:checkbox   :image     :radio      :text
:file       :input     :reset
```

Element state filters

```
:animated   :disabled  :hidden     :visible
:checked    :enabled   :selected
```

Selection position filters

```
:eq(n)      :first     :last       :nth(n)
:even       :gt(n)     :lt(n)      :odd
```

Document position filters

```
:first-child        :nth-child(n)
:last-child         :nth-child(even)
:only-child         :nth-child(odd)
                    :nth-child(xn+y)
```

Miscellaneous filters

```
:contains(text)     :not(selector)
:empty              :parent
:has(selector)
```

Basic Methods and Properties

These are the basic methods and properties of jQuery objects.
They don't alter the selection or the selected elements in any
way, but they allow you to query and iterate over the set of

selected elements. See the section "Queries and Query Results" on page 8 for details.

context
> The context, or root element, under which the selection was made. This is the second argument to `$()` or the Document object.

each(*f(idx,elt)*)
> Invokes *f* once as a method of each selected element. Stops iterating if the function returns `false`. Returns the jQuery object on which it was invoked.

get(*idx*):elt
get():array
> Return the selected element at the specified index in the jQuery object. You can also use regular square bracket array indexing. With no arguments, `get()` is a synonym for `toArray()`.

index():int
index(*sel*):int
index(*elt*):int
> With no argument, return the index of the first selected element among its siblings. With a selector argument, return the index of the first selected element within the set of elements that match the selector *sel*, or -1 if it is not found. With an element argument, return the index of *elt* in the selected elements, or -1 if it is not found.

is(*sel*):boolean
> Returns `true` if at least one of the selected elements also matches *sel*.

length
> The number of selected elements.

map(*f(idx,elt)*):jQuery
> Invokes *f* once as a method of each selected element, and returns a new jQuery object that holds the returned values, with `null` and `undefined` values omitted and array values flattened.

---

selector
> The selector string originally passed to $().

size():int
> Returns the value of the length property.

toArray():array
> Returns a true array of the selected elements.

Selection Methods

The methods described in this section alter the set of selected elements by filtering them, adding new elements, or by using the selected elements as starting points for new selections. In jQuery 1.4 and later, jQuery selections are always sorted in document order and do not contain duplicates. See "Selection Methods" on page 95.

add(*sel*, [*context*])
add(*elts*)
add(*html*)
> The arguments to add() are passed to $(), and the resulting selection is merged with the current selection.

andSelf()
> Adds the previously selected set of elements (from the stack) to the selection.

children([*sel*])
> Selects children of the selected elements. With no argument, selects all children. With a selector, selects only matching children.

closest(*sel*, [*context*])
> Selects the closest ancestor of each selected element that matches *sel* and is a descendant of *context*. If *context* is omitted, the context property of the jQuery object is used.

contents()
> Selects all children of each selected element, including text nodes and comments.

`end()`

> Pops the internal stack, restoring the selection to the state it was in before the last selection-altering method.

`eq(idx)`

> Selects only the selected element with the specified index. In jQuery 1.4, negative indexes count from the end.

`filter(sel)`
`filter(elts)`
`filter(f(idx):boolean)`

> Filter the selection so it only includes elements that also match the selector *sel*, that are included in the array-like object *elts*, or for which the predicate *f* returns **true** when invoked as a method of the element.

`find(sel)`

> Selects all descendants of any selected element that match *sel*.

`first()`

> Selects only the first selected element.

`has(sel)`
`has(elt)`

> Filter the selection to include only those selected elements that have a descendant that matches *sel* or that are ancestors of *elt*.

`last()`

> Selects only the last selected element.

`next([sel])`

> Selects the next sibling of each selected element. If *sel* is specified, excludes those that do not match.

`nextAll([sel])`

> Selects all of the siblings following each selected element. If *sel* is specified, excludes those that do not match.

`nextUntil(sel)`

> Selects the siblings following each selected element up to (but not including) the first sibling that matches *sel*.

---

not(*sel*)
not(*elts*)
not(*f(idx)*:boolean)

This is the opposite of **filter()**. It filters the selection to exclude elements that match *sel*, that are included in *elts*, or for which *f* returns **true**. *elts* may be a single element or an array-like object of elements. *f* is invoked as a method of each selected element.

offsetParent()

Selects the nearest positioned ancestor of each selected element.

parent([*sel*])

Selects the parent of each selected element. If *sel* is specified, excludes any that do not match.

parents([*sel*])

Selects the ancestors of each selected element. If *sel* is specified, excludes any that do not match.

parentsUntil(*sel*)

Selects the ancestors of each selected element up to (but not including) the first one that matches *sel*.

prev([*sel*])

Selects the previous sibling of each selected element. If *sel* is specified, excludes those that do not match.

prevAll([*sel*])

Selects all of the siblings before each selected element. If *sel* is specified, excludes those that do not match.

prevUntil(*sel*)

Selects the siblings preceding each selected element up to (but not including) the first sibling that matches *sel*.

pushStack(*elts*)

Pushes the current state of the selection so that it can be restored with **end()**, and then selects the elements in the *elts* array (or array-like object).

```
siblings([sel])
```
> Selects the siblings of each selected element, excluding the element itself. If *sel* is specified, excludes any siblings that do not match.

```
slice(startidx, [endidx])
```
> Filters the selection to include only elements with an index greater than or equal to *startidx*, and less than (but not equal to) *endidx*. Negative indexes count backward from the end of the selection. If *endidx* is omitted, the `length` property is used.

Element Methods

The methods described here query and set the HTML attributes and CSS style properties of elements. Setter callback functions with an argument named *current* are passed the current value of whatever it is they are computing a new value for; see Chapter 2.

```
addClass(names)
addClass(f(idx,current):names)
```
> Add the specified CSS class name (or names) to the `class` attribute of each selected element. Or, invoke *f* as a method of each element to compute the class name or names to add.

```
attr(name):value
attr(name, value)
attr(name, f(idx,current):value)
attr(obj)
```
> With one string argument, return the value of the named attribute for the first selected element. With two arguments, set the named attribute of all selected elements to the specified *value*, or invoke *f* as a method of each element to compute a value. With a single object argument, use property names as attribute names, and property values as attribute values or attribute computing functions.

```
css(name):value
css(name, value)
css(name, f(idx,current):value)
css(obj)
```
> Like `attr()`, but query or set CSS style attributes instead
> of HTML attributes.

```
data():obj
data(key):value
data(key, value)
data(obj)
```
> With no arguments, return the data object for the first
> selected element. With one string argument, return the
> value of the named property of that data object. With two
> arguments, set the named property of the data object of
> all selected elements to the specified *value*. With one ob-
> ject argument, replace the data object of all selected
> elements.

```
hasClass(name):boolean
```
> Returns `true` if any of the selected elements includes
> *name* in its `class` attribute.

```
height():int
height(h)
height(f(idx,current):int)
```
> Return the height (not including padding, border, or mar-
> gin) of the first selected element, or set the height of all
> selected elements to *h* or to the value computed by invok-
> ing *f* as a method of each element.

```
innerHeight():int
```
> Returns the height plus padding of the first selected
> element.

```
innerWidth():int
```
> Returns the width plus padding of the first selected
> element.

`offset():coords`
`offset(coords)`
`offset(f(idx,current):coords)`

> Return the X and Y position (in document coordinates) of
> the first selected element, or set the position of all selected
> elements to *coords* or to the value computed by invoking
> *f* as a method of each element. Coordinates are specified
> as objects with `top` and `left` properties.

`offsetParent():jQuery`

> Selects the nearest positioned ancestor of each selected
> element and returns them in a new jQuery object.

`outerHeight([margins=false]):int`

> Returns the height plus the padding and border, and, if
> *margins* is `true`, the margins of the first selected element.

`outerWidth([margins=false]):int`

> Returns the width plus the padding and border, and, if
> *margins* is `true`, the margins of the first selected element.

`position():coords`

> Returns the position of the first selected element relative
> to its nearest positioned ancestor. The return value is an
> object with `top` and `left` properties.

`removeAttr(name)`

> Removes the named attribute from all selected elements.

`removeClass(names)`
`removeClass(f(idx,current):names)`

> Remove the specified name (or names) from the `class` at-
> tribute of all selected elements. If a function is passed in-
> stead of a string, invoke it as a method of each element to
> compute the name to be removed.

`removeData([key])`

> Removes the named property from the data object of each
> selected element. If no property name is specified, re-
> moves the entire data object instead.

```
scrollLeft():int
scrollLeft(int)
```
Return the horizontal scrollbar position of the first selected element or set it for all selected elements.

```
scrollTop():int
scrollTop(int)
```
Return the vertical scrollbar position of the first selected element or set it for all selected elements.

```
toggleClass(names, [add])
toggleClass(f(idx,current):names, [add])
```
Toggle the specified class name (or names) in the `class` property of each selected element. If *f* is specified, invoke it as a method of each selected element to compute the name to be toggled. If *add* is `true` or `false`, add or remove the class names rather than toggling them.

```
val():value
val(value)
val(f(idx,current)):value
```
Return the form value or selection state of the first selected element, or set the value or selection state of all selected elements to *value* or to the value computed by invoking *f* as a method of each element.

```
width():int
width(w)
width(f(idx,current):int)
```
Return the width (not including padding, border, or margin) of the first selected element, or set the width of all selected elements to *w* or to the value computed by invoking *f* as a method of each element.

Insertion and Deletion Methods

The methods described here insert, delete, and replace document content. In the method signatures below, the *content* argument may be a jQuery object, a string of HTML, or an individual document element, and the *target* argument may be a jQuery object, an individual document element, or a selector string. See "Getting and Setting Element Content" on page 18 and Chapter 3 for further details.

`after(content)`
`after(f(idx):content)`

> Insert *content* after each selected element, or invoke *f* as a method of—and insert its return value after—each selected element.

`append(content)`
`append(f(idx,html):content)`

> Append *content* to each selected element, or invoke *f* as a method of—and append its return value to—each selected element.

`appendTo(target):jQuery`

> Appends the selected elements to the end of each specified *target* element, cloning them as necessary if there is more than one target.

`before(content)`
`before(f(idx):content)`

> Like `after()`, but make insertions before the selected elements.

`clone([data=false]):jQuery`

> Makes a deep copy of each of the selected elements and returns a new jQuery object representing the cloned elements. If *data* is **true**, also clones the data (including event handlers) associated with the selected elements.

`detach([sel])`

> Like `remove()`, but does not delete any data associated with the detached elements.

`empty()`

> Deletes the content of all selected elements.

`html():string`
`html(htmlText)`
`html(f(idx,current):htmlText)`

> With no arguments, return the content of the first selected element as an HTML-formatted string. With one

argument, set the content of all selected elements to the specified *htmlText* or to the value returned by invoking *f* as a method of those elements.

insertAfter(*target*):jQuery

Inserts the selected elements after each *target* element, cloning them as necessary if there is more than one target.

insertBefore(*target*):jQuery

Inserts the selected elements before each *target* element, cloning them as necessary if there is more than one target.

prepend(*content*)
prepend(*f(idx,html)*:content)

Like append(), but insert content at the beginning of each selected element.

prependTo(*target*):jQuery

Like appendTo(), except that the selected elements are inserted at the beginning of the target elements.

remove([*sel*])

Removes all selected elements, or all selected elements that also match *sel*, from the document, as well as any data (including event handlers) associated with them. Note that the removed elements are no longer part of the document, but are still members of the returned jQuery object.

replaceAll(*target*)

Inserts the selected elements into the document so that they replace each *target* element, cloning the selected elements as needed if there is more than one target.

replaceWith(*content*)
replaceWith(*f(idx,html)*:content)

Replace each selected element with *content*, or invoke *f* as a method of each selected element—passing the element index and current HTML content—and then replace that element with the return value.

text():string
text(*plainText*)
text(*f(idx,current)*:plainText)

> With no arguments, return the content of the first selected element as a plain-text string. With one argument, set the content of all selected elements to the specified *plain Text* or to the value returned by invoking *f* as a method of those elements.

unwrap()

> Removes the parent of each selected element, replacing it with the selected element and its siblings.

wrap(*wrapper*)
wrap(*f(idx)*:wrapper)

> Wrap *wrapper* around each selected element, cloning as needed if there is more than one selected element. If a function is passed, invoke it as a method of each selected element to compute the wrapper. The *wrapper* may be an element, a jQuery object, a selector, or a string of HTML, but it must have a single innermost element.

wrapAll(*wrapper*)

> Wraps *wrapper* around the selected elements as a group by inserting wrapper at the location of the first selected element and then copying all selected elements into the innermost element of *wrapper*.

wrapInner(*wrapper*)
wrapInner(*f(idx)*:wrapper)

> Like wrap(), but inserts *wrapper* (or the return value of *f*) around the content of each selected element rather than around the elements themselves.

Event Methods

The methods in this section are for registering event handlers and triggering events; see Chapter 4.

event-type()
event-type(*f(event)*)

> Register *f* as a handler for *event-type*, or trigger an event of *event-type*. jQuery defines the following convenience methods that follow this pattern:

ajaxComplete	blur	focusin	mousedown	mouseup
ajaxError	change	focusout	mouseenter	resize
ajaxSend	click	keydown	mouseleave	scroll
ajaxStart	dblclick	keypress	mousemove	select
ajaxStop	error	keyup	mouseout	submit
ajaxSuccess	focus	load	mouseover	unload

bind(*type*, [*data*], *f(event)*)
bind(*events*)

> Register *f* as a handler for events of the specified *type* on each of the selected elements. If *data* is specified, add it to the event object before invoking *f*. *type* may specify multiple event types and may include namespaces.

> If a single object is passed, treat it as a mapping of event types to handler functions, and register handlers for all the specified events on each selected element.

delegate(*sel*, *type*, [*data*], *f(event)*)

> Registers *f* as a live event handler. *f* will be triggered when events of type *type* occur on an element matching *sel* and bubble up to any of the selected elements. If *data* is specified, it will be added to the event object before *f* is invoked.

die(*type*, [*f(event)*])

> Deregisters live event handlers registered with live() for events of type *type* on elements that match the selector string of the current selection. If a specific event handler function *f* is specified, only deregister that one.

hover(*f(event)*)
hover(*enter(event)*, *leave(event)*)

> Register event handlers for "mouseenter" and "mouseleave" events on all selected elements. If only one function is specified, it is used as the handler for both events.

`live(type, [data], f(event))`

> Registers *f* as a live event handler for events of type *type*. If *data* is specified, adds it to the event object before invoking *f*. This method does not use the set of selected elements, but it does use the selector string and context object of the jQuery object. *f* will be triggered when *type* events bubble up to the context object (usually the document) and the event's target element matches the selector. See `delegate()`.

`one(type, [data], f(event))`
`one(events)`

> Like `bind()`, except that the registered event handlers are automatically deregistered after they are invoked once.

`ready(f())`

> Registers *f* to be invoked when the document becomes ready, or invokes it immediately if the document is ready. This method does not use the selected elements and is a synonym for `$(f)`.

`toggle(f1(event), f2(event),...)`

> Registers a "click" event handler on all selected elements that alternate (or toggle) among the specified handler functions.

`trigger(type, [params])`
`trigger(event)`

> Trigger a *type* event on all selected elements, passing *params* as extra parameters to event handlers. *params* may be omitted, or may be a single value or an array of values. If you pass an *event* object, its `type` property specifies the event type, and any other properties are copied into the event object that is passed to the handlers.

`triggerHandler(type, [params])`

> Like `trigger()`, but does not allow the triggered event to bubble or to trigger the browser's default action.

`unbind([type],[f(event)])`

> With no arguments, deregisters all jQuery event handlers on all selected elements. With one argument, deregisters

all event handlers for the *type* events on all selected elements. With two arguments, deregisters *f* as a handler for *type* events on all selected elements. *type* may name multiple event types and may include namespaces.

`undelegate()`
`undelegate(sel, type, [f(event)])`

With no arguments, deregister all live event handlers delegated from the selected elements. With two arguments, deregister live event handlers for *type* events on elements matching *sel* that are delegated from the selected elements. With three arguments, only deregister the single handler *f*.

Effects and Animation Methods

The methods described here produce visual effects and custom animations. Most return the jQuery object on which they are called; see Chapter 5.

Animation options

```
complete  duration  easing  queue  specialEasing step
```

`jQuery.fx.off`

Disables all effects and animations when set to **true**.

`animate(props, opts)`

Animates the CSS properties specified by the *props* object on each selected element, using the options specified by *opts*. See "Custom Animations" on page 53 for details of both objects.

`animate(props, [duration], [easing], [f()])`

Animates the CSS properties specified by *props* on each selected element, using the specified *duration* and *easing* function. Invokes *f* as a method of each selected element when done.

`clearQueue([qname="fx"])`

Clears the effects queue or the named queue for each selected element.

```
delay(duration, [qname="fx"])
```
Adds a delay of the specified duration to the effects queue or the named queue.

```
dequeue([qname="fx"])
```
Removes and invokes the next function on the effects queue or the named queue. It is not normally necessary to dequeue the effects queue.

```
fadeIn([duration=400],[f()])
fadeOut([duration=400],[f()])
```
Fade the selected elements in or out by animating their opacity for *duration* ms. When complete, invoke *f*, if specified, as a method of each selected element.

```
fadeTo(duration, opacity, [f()])
```
Animates the CSS opacity of the selected elements to *opacity* over the specified *duration*. When complete, invokes *f*, if specified, as a method of each selected element.

```
hide()
hide(duration, [f()])
```
With no arguments, hide each selected element immediately. Otherwise, animate the size and opacity of each selected element so that they are hidden after *duration* ms. When complete, invoke *f*, if specified, as a method of each selected element.

```
slideDown([duration=400],[f()])
slideUp([duration=400],[f()])
slideToggle([duration=400],[f()])
```
Show, hide, or toggle the visibility of each selected element by animating its height for the specified *duration*. When complete, invoke *f*, if specified, as a method of each selected element.

```
show()
show(duration, [f()])
```
With no arguments, show each selected element immediately. Otherwise, animate the size and opacity of each selected element so that they are fully visible after

---

duration ms. When complete, invoke *f*, if specified, as a method of each selected element.

stop([*clear*=false], [*jump*=false])

Stops the current animation (if one is running) on all selected elements. If *clear* is true, also clears the effects queue for each element. If *jump* is true, jumps the animation to its final value before stopping it.

toggle([*show*])
toggle(*duration*, [*f*()])

If *show* is true, show() the selected elements immediately. If *show* is false, hide() the selected elements immediately. If *show* is omitted, toggle the visibility of the elements.

If *duration* is specified, toggle the visibility of the selected elements with a size and opacity animation of the specified length. When complete, invoke *f*, if specified, as a method of each selected element.

queue([*qname*="fx"]):array
queue([*qname*="fx"], *f*(next))
queue([*qname*="fx"], *newq*)

With no arguments or just a queue name, return the named queue of the first selected element. With a function argument, add *f* to the named queue of all selected elements. With an array argument, replace the named queue of all selected elements with the *newq* array of functions.

Ajax Functions

Most of the jQuery Ajax-related functionality takes the form of utility functions rather than methods. These are some of the most complicated functions in the jQuery library; see Chapter 6 for complete details.

Ajax status codes

    success error notmodified timeout parsererror

Ajax Data Types

    text html xml script json jsonp

Ajax Events

ajaxStart	ajaxSuccess	ajaxComplete
ajaxSend	ajaxError	ajaxStop

Ajax Options

async	data	jsonp	timeout
beforeSend	dataFilter	jsonpCallback	traditional
cache	dataType	password	type
complete	error	processData	url
contentType	global	scriptCharset	username
context	ifModified	success	xhr

`jQuery.ajax(options):XHR`

This is the complicated but fully general Ajax function on which all of jQuery's Ajax utilities are based. It expects a single object argument whose properties specify all details of the Ajax request and the handling of the server's response. The most common options are described in "Common Options" on page 73, and callback options are covered in "Callbacks" on page 75.

`jQuery.ajaxSetup(options)`

Sets default values for jQuery's Ajax options. Passes the same kind of options object you would pass to `jQuery.ajax()`. The values you specify will be used by any subsequent Ajax request that does not specify the value itself. This function has no return value.

`jQuery.getJSON(url, [data], [f(object,status)]):XHR`

Asynchronously requests the specified *url*, adding any *data* that is specified. When the response is received, parses it as JSON, and passes the resulting object to the callback function *f*. Returns the XMLHttpRequest object, if any, used for the request.

`jQuery.getScript(url, [f(text,status)]):XHR`

Asynchronously requests the specified *url*. When the response arrives, executes it as a script, and then passes the response text to *f*. Returns the XMLHttpRequest object, if any, used for the request. Cross-domains are allowed, but does not pass the script text to *f*, and does not return an XMLHttpRequest object.

`jQuery.get(url,[data],[f(data,status,xhr)],[type]):XHR`

Makes an asynchronous HTTP GET request for *url*, adding *data*, if any, to the query parameter portion of that URL. When the response arrives, interprets it as data of the specified *type*—or according to the Content-Type header of the response—and executes it or parses it if necessary. Finally, passes the (possibly parsed) response data to the callback *f* along with the jQuery status code and the XMLHttpRequest object used for the request. That XMLHttpRequest object, if any, is also the return value of `jQuery.get()`.

`jQuery.post(url,[data],[f(data,status,xhr)],[type]):XHR`

Like `jQuery.get()`, but makes an HTTP POST request instead of a GET request.

`jQuery.param(o, [old=false]):string`

Serializes the names and values of the properties of *o* in www-form-urlencoded form, suitable for adding to a URL or passing as the body of an HTTP POST request. Most jQuery Ajax functions will do this automatically for you if you pass an object as the *data* parameter. Pass true as the second argument if you want jQuery 1.3-style shallow serialization.

`jQuery.parseJSON(text):object`

Parses JSON-formatted *text* and returns the resulting object. jQuery's Ajax functions use this function internally when you request JSON-encoded data.

`load(url, [data], [f(text,status,xhr)])`

Asynchronously requests the *url*, adding any *data* that is specified. When the response arrives, interprets it as a string of HTML and inserts it into each selected element, replacing any existing content. Finally, invokes *f* as a method of each selected element, passing the response text, the jQuery status code, and the XMLHttpRequest object used for the request.

If *url* includes a space, any text after the space is used as a selector, and only the portions of the response document that match that selector are inserted into the selected elements.

Unlike most jQuery Ajax utilities, `load()` is a method not a function. Like most jQuery methods, it returns the jQuery object on which it was invoked.

`serialize():string`
> Serializes the names and values of the selected forms and form elements, returning a string in `www-form-urlencoded` format.

Utility Functions

These are miscellaneous jQuery functions and properties (not methods); see Chapter 7 for more details.

`jQuery.boxModel`
> A deprecated synonym for `jQuery.support.boxModel`.

`jQuery.browser`
> This property refers to an object that identifies the browser vendor and version. The object has the property `msie` for Internet Explorer, `mozilla` for Firefox, `webkit` for Safari and Chrome, and `opera` for Opera. The `version` property is the browser version number.

`jQuery.contains(a,b):boolean`
> Returns true if document element *a* contains element *b*.

`jQuery.data(elt):data`
`jQuery.data(elt, key):value`
`jQuery.data(elt, data)`
`jQuery.data(elt, key, value)`
> A low-level version of the `data()` method. With one element argument, return the data object for that element. With an element and a string, return the named value from that element's data object. With an element and an object, set the data object for the element. With an element, string, and value, set the named value in the element's data object.

`jQuery.dequeue(elt, [qname="fx"])`

Removes and invokes the first function in the named queue of the specified element. It is the same as `$(elt).dequeue(qname)`.

`jQuery.each(o, f(name,value)):o`
`jQuery.each(a, f(index,value)):a`

Invoke *f* once for each property of *o*, passing the name and value of the property and invoking *f* as a method of the value. If the first argument is an array or array-like object, invoke *f* as a method of each element in the array, passing the array index and element value as arguments. Iteration stops if *f* returns `false`. This function returns its first argument.

`jQuery.error(msg)`

Throws an exception containing *msg*. You can call this function from plugins or override (e.g., `jQuery.error = alert`) it when debugging.

`jQuery.extend(obj):object`
`jQuery.extend([deep=false], target, obj...):object`

With one argument, copy the properties of *obj* into the global `jQuery` namespace. With two or more arguments, copy the properties of the second and subsequent objects, in order, into the *target* object. If the optional *deep* argument is `true`, a deep copy is done and properties are copied recursively. The return value is the object that was extended.

`jQuery.globalEval(code):void`

Executes the specified JavaScript *code* as if it were a top-level `<script>`. No return value.

`jQuery.grep(a, f(elt,idx):boolean, [invert=false]):array`

Returns a new array that contains only the elements of *a* for which *f* returns `true`. Or, if *invert* is `true`, returns only those elements for which *f* returns `false`.

`jQuery.inArray(v, a):integer`

Searches the array or array-like object *a* for an element *v*, and returns the index at which it is found or -1.

`jQuery.isArray(x):boolean`

Returns **true** only if *x* is a true JavaScript array.

`jQuery.isEmptyObject(x):boolean`

Return s**true** only if *x* has no enumerable properties.

`jQuery.isFunction(x):boolean`

Returns **true** only if *x* is a JavaScript function.

`jQuery.isPlainObject(x):boolean`

Returns **true** only if *x* is a plain JavaScript object, such as one created by an object literal.

`jQuery.isXMLDoc(x):true`

Returns **true** only if *x* is an XML document or an element of an XML document.

`jQuery.makeArray(a):array`

Returns a new JavaScript array that contains the same elements as the array-like object *a*.

`jQuery.map(a, f(elt, idx)):array`

Returns a new array that contains the values returned by *f* when invoked for each element in the array (or array-like object) *a*. Returned values of **null** are ignored, and returned arrays are flattened.

`jQuery.merge(a,b):array`

Appends the elements of the array *b* to *a*, and returns *a*. The arguments may be array-like objects or true arrays.

`jQuery.noConflict([radical=false])`

Restores the symbol **$** to its value before the jQuery library was loaded, and returns **jQuery**. If *radical* is true, also restores the value of the **jQuery** symbol.

`jQuery.proxy(f, o):function`
`jQuery.proxy(o, name):function`

Return a function that invokes *f* as a method of *o*, or a function that invokes *o*[*name*] as a method of *o*.

`jQuery.queue(elt, [qname="fx"], [f])`

Queries or sets the named queue of *elt*, or adds a new function *f* to that queue; same as **$(elt).queue(qname, f)**.

`jQuery.removeData(elt, [name]):void`

    Removes the named property from the data object of *elt*, or removes the data object itself.

`jQuery.support`

    An object containing a number of properties describing the features and bugs of the current browser. Most are of interest only to plugin writers. `jQuery.support.boxModel` is false in IE browsers running in quirks mode.

`jQuery.trim(s):string`

    Returns a copy of the string *s*, with leading and trailing whitespace trimmed off.

Index

We'd like to hear your suggestions for improving our indexes. Send email to
index@oreilly.com.

J

jQuery
  defined, 2
  documentation, 8
  obtaining and including in
    web pages, 4
jQuery ( ) function, 3, 4–8, 114
  defined, 7
  invoking, 5
jquery property, 10
jQuery UI library, 109
jQuery.ajax( ) function, 63, 72,
    132
  callbacks, 76
  common options, 73
  uncommon options and
    hooks, 78
jQuery.ajaxSetup( ) function,
    132
jQuery.boxModel property, 134
jQuery.browser property, 83,
    134
jQuery.contains( ) function, 84,
    134
jQuery.data( ) function, 134
jQuery.dequeue( ) function, 135
jQuery.each( ) function, 84, 135
jQuery.easing object, 57
jQuery.error( ) function, 135
jQuery.event.trigger( ) function,
    43
jQuery.expr object, adding
    properties to, 106
jQuery.extend( ) function, 84,
    135
jQuery.fn object, 103
jQuery.fx.off property, 50, 129
jQuery.fx.speeds, 49, 56
jQuery.get( ) and jQuery.post( )
    functions, 70, 133
  options, 73
jQuery.getJSON( ) function, 68,
    132
jQuery.getScript( ) function, 66,
    132

jQuery.globalEval( ) function, 85,
    135
jQuery.grep( ) function, 85, 135
jQuery.inArray( ) function, 85,
    135
jQuery.isArray( ) function, 85,
    136
jQuery.isEmptyObject( )
    function, 85, 136
jQuery.isFunction( ) function, 86,
    136
jQuery.isPlainObject( ) function,
    86, 136
jQuery.isXMLDoc( ) function,
    136
jQuery.makeArray( ) function,
    86, 136
jQuery.map( ) function, 86, 136
jQuery.merge( ) function, 86,
    136
jQuery.noConflict( ) function, 6,
    136
jQuery.param( ) function, 69,
    133
jQuery.parseJSON( ) function,
    87, 133
jQuery.proxy( ) function, 87, 136
jQuery.queue( ) function, 136
jQuery.removeData( ) function,
    137
jQuery.support( ) function, 87,
    137
jQuery.trim( ) function, 87, 137
JSON (JavaScript Object
    Notation)
  jQuery.getJSON( ) function,
    68, 132
  jQuery.parseJSON( )
    function, 87, 133
json data type (Ajax), 71
JSONP, 68
jsonp data type (Ajax), 72
jsonp option (Ajax), 79
jsonpCallback option (Ajax), 79

Related Titles from O'Reilly

Web Programming

ActionScript 3.0 Cookbook

ActionScript 3.0 Design Patterns

ActionScript for Flash MX: The Definitive Guide, *2nd Edition*

Adobe AIR 1.5 Cookbook

Adobe AIR for JavaScript Developer's Pocket Guide

Advanced Rails

Ajax Design Patterns

Ajax Hacks

Ajax on Rails

Ajax: The Definitive Guide

Apache 2 Pocket Reference

Apache Cookbook, *2nd Edition*

Building Scalable Web Sites

Designing Web Navigation

Dojo: The Definitive Guide

Dynamic HTML: The Definitive Reference, *3rd Edition*

Essential ActionScript 3.0

Essential PHP Security

Ferret

Flash CS4: The Missing Manual

Flash Hacks

Head First HTML with CSS & XHTML

Head First JavaScript

Head First PHP & MySQL

High Performance Web Sites

HTTP: The Definitive Guide

JavaScript & DHTML Cookbook, *2nd Edition*

JavaScript Pocket Reference, *2nd Edition*

JavaScript: The Definitive Guide, *5th Edition*

JavaScript: The Good Parts

JavaScript: The Missing Manual

Learning ActionScript 3.0

Learning PHP and MySQL, *2nd Edition*

PHP Cookbook, *2nd Edition*

PHP Hacks

PHP in a Nutshell

PHP Pocket Reference, *2nd Edition*

Programming ColdFusion MX, *2nd Edition*

Programming Flex 2

Programming PHP, *2nd Edition*

Programming Amazon Web Services

Rails Cookbook

The ActionScript 3.0 Quick Reference Guide

Twitter API: Up and Running

Universal Design for Web Applications

Upgrading to PHP 5

Web Database Applications with PHP and MySQL, *2nd Edition*

Website Optimization

Web Site Cookbook

Webmaster in a Nutshell, *3rd Edition*

O'REILLY®

Our books are available at most retail and online bookstores.

To order direct: 1-800-998-9938 • *order@oreilly.com* • *www.oreilly.com*

Online editions of most O'Reilly Titles are available by subscription at *safari.oreilly.com*

Get even more for your money.

Join the O'Reilly Community, and register the O'Reilly books you own. It's free, and you'll get:

- $4.99 ebook upgrade offer
- 40% upgrade offer on O'Reilly print books
- Membership discounts on books and events
- Free lifetime updates to ebooks and videos
- Multiple ebook formats, DRM FREE
- Participation in the O'Reilly community
- Newsletters
- Account management
- 100% Satisfaction Guarantee

Registering your books is easy:

1. Go to: oreilly.com/go/register
2. Create an O'Reilly login.
3. Provide your address.
4. Register your books.

Note: English-language books only

To order books online:
oreilly.com/store

For questions about products or an order:
orders@oreilly.com

To sign up to get topic-specific email announcements and/or news about upcoming books, conferences, special offers, and new technologies:
elists@oreilly.com

For technical questions about book content:
booktech@oreilly.com

To submit new book proposals to our editors:
proposals@oreilly.com

O'Reilly books are available in multiple DRM-free ebook formats. For more information:
oreilly.com/ebooks

O'REILLY®

Spreading the knowledge of innovators   oreilly.com